SEVEN SEAS ENTERTA

THE VILLAIN DEMON KNIGHT Vol. 1

story by NEKOTA   art by SEIKAN   character design by ASAHIKO

TRANSLATION
M. Jean

ADAPTATION
Molly Muldoon

LETTERING
Giuseppe A. Fusco

COVER DESIGN
H. Qi

PROOFREADER
Dave Murray

COPY EDITOR
B. Lillian Martin

EDITOR
K. McDonald

PRODUCTION DESIGNER
Christina McKenzie

PRODUCTION MANAGER
Lissa Pattillo

PREPRESS TECHNICIAN
Melanie Ujimori
Jules Valera

EDITOR-IN-CHIEF
Julie Davis

ASSOCIATE PUBLISHER
Adam Arnold

PUBLISHER
Jason DeAngelis

ISBN: 978-1-63858-896-2
Printed in Canada
First Printing: March 2022
10 9 8 7 6 5 4 3 2 1

READING DIRECTIONS

This book reads from *right to left*, Japanese style. If this is your first time reading manga, you start reading from the top right panel on each page and take it from there. If you get lost, just follow the numbered diagram here. It may seem backwards at first, but you'll get the hang of it! Have fun!!

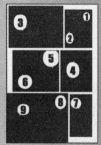

Follow us online: www.SevenSeasEntertainment.com

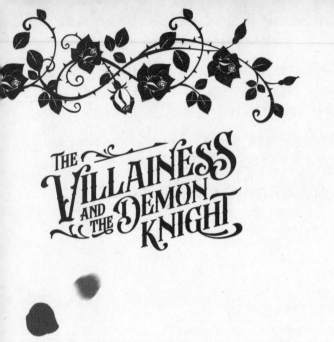

THE VILLAINESS AND THE DEMON KNIGHT

SEIKAN

This is my first serialization
and my first volume!
You truly never know what
life will bring. I'll do my best
to show you lots of this
beautiful world!

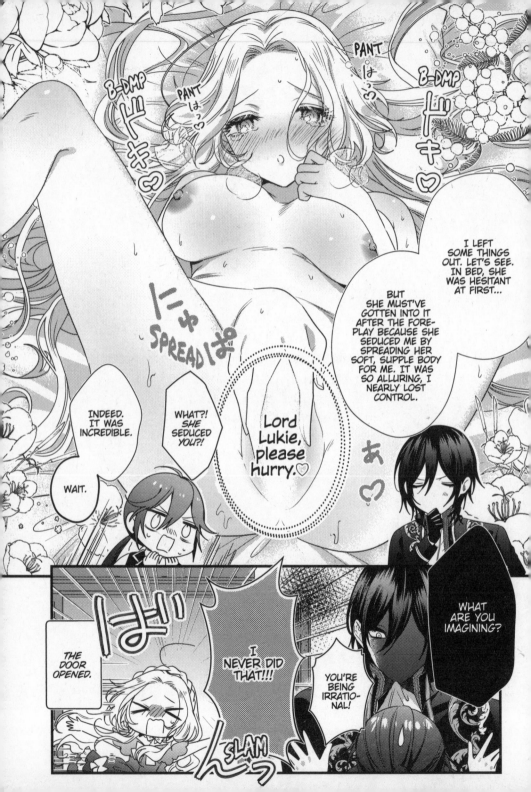

PANT

PANT

B-DMP

B-DMP

SPREAD

I LEFT SOME THINGS OUT. LET'S SEE. IN BED, SHE WAS HESITANT AT FIRST...

BUT SHE MUST'VE GOTTEN INTO IT AFTER THE FORE-PLAY BECAUSE SHE SEDUCED ME BY SPREADING HER SOFT, SUPPLE BODY FOR ME. IT WAS SO ALLURING, I NEARLY LOST CONTROL.

INDEED. IT WAS INCREDIBLE.

WHAT?! SHE SEDUCED YOU?!

Lord Lukie, please hurry. ♡

WAIT.

WHAT ARE YOU IMAGINING?

THE DOOR OPENED.

I NEVER DID THAT!!!

YOU'RE BEING IRRATIO-NAL!

SLAM

IF I WERE TO LIST EVERY AMAZING THING ABOUT HER, FIRST WOULD BE HER FACE. WHILE STILL YOUTHFUL, IT IS BLOSSOMING AND BEAUTIFUL. THE VOICE THAT COMES FROM THOSE GLOSSY PLUMP LIPS IS LIKE BIRDSONG, OR BELLS.

THOSE FRAGILE, SUPPLE, FAIR-SKINNED ARMS MAKE ME WANT TO PROTECT HER AND WORRY FOR HER. HER AMBER HAIR GLEAMS LIKE SILK AND LOOKS NEARLY TRANSLUCENT WHEN IT CATCHES THE SUN. WHEN THE WIND MAKES IT RIPPLE, IT'S AS IF THE SWEET SCENT OF FLOWERS IS WAFTING IN THE AIR. WHAT A STIMULUS! SHE'S LIKE A GODDESS. A GODDESS AMONG GODDESSES.

AT A GLANCE, HER DIGNIFIED APPEARANCE MAKES HER LOOK UNAPPROACHABLE, BUT WHEN SHE SMILES, SHE'S AS LOVELY AND INVITING AS A BLOOMING FLOWER.

SHE'S ALSO HIGHLY EDUCATED, HAVING RECEIVED CONSORT TRAINING. SHE'S BEEN POLISHED ALL THE WAY TO HER FINGERTIPS. SHE COULD CHARM ANYONE SHE MEETS. AT THIS RATE, I WANT TO KEEP HER SHUT AWAY FROM NOT ONLY THE SECOND PRINCE, BUT EVERY OTHER MAN.

BLAB

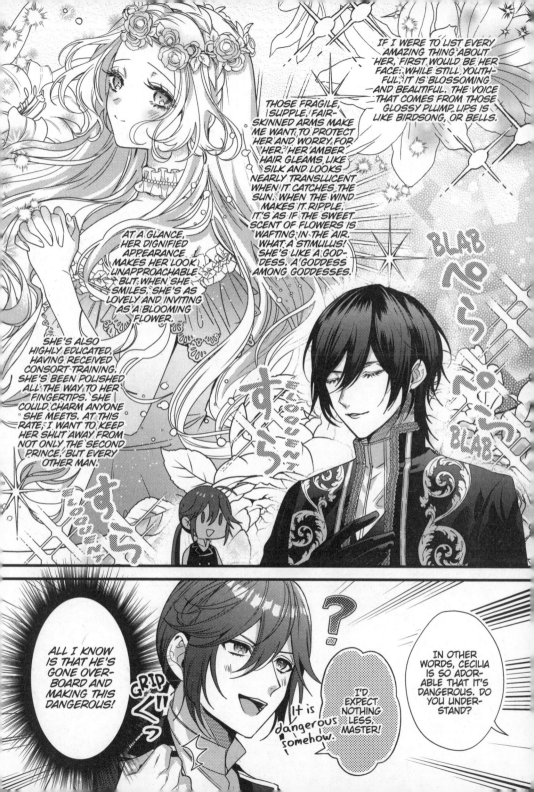

ALL I KNOW IS THAT HE'S GONE OVERBOARD AND MAKING THIS DANGEROUS!

GRIP

It is dangerous somehow.

?

I'D EXPECT NOTHING LESS, MASTER!

IN OTHER WORDS, CECILIA IS SO ADORABLE THAT IT'S DANGEROUS. DO YOU UNDERSTAND?

THIS IS THE KINGDOM OF BERN, A WORLD MUCH LIKE THOSE IN FANTASY STORIES, WHERE SWORDS AND MAGIC ARE COMMONPLACE.

NATURALLY, CONVENIENT PLOT TWISTS ARE ALSO COMMON-PLACE.

BAM

Compliment Lady Cecilia or you cannot leave this room.

A TIME-OUT ROOM WHERE WE MUST COMPLIMENT LADY CECILIA OR WE CAN'T GET OUT?!

I MADE A MISTAKE. SORRY. (OMNIPOTENT VOICE.)

SHOCK

FINN

No cheat codes for this one.

MASTER, WHY ARE YOU STUCK IN HERE WITH ME?!

SHOULDN'T YOU BE STUCK IN A ROOM WITH HER?

WAIT. THE BED IN HERE IS POINTLESS. THIS ANGERS ME GREATLY!

And there's only one!

MAS-TER!

CALM DOWN, FINN. LEAVE THIS TO ME.

Bonus

Afterword

Thank you so much for picking up the manga adaptation of The Villainess and the Demon Knight. Starting next volume, the setting will move from the brothel to the Herbst Manor. I hope you'll look forward to it!

Seikan

☆ SPECIAL THANKS ☆

♡ Story: Nekota-sensei

♡ Character design: Asahiko-sensei

♡ Everyone at the Zero-Sum editorial department

♡ Everyone involved with the publishing and sale of this volume

♡ All of my readers

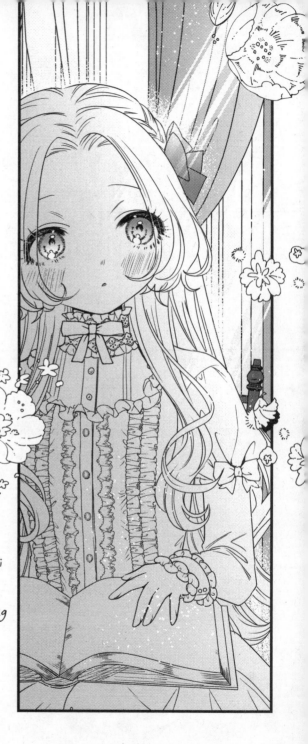

THE VILLAINESS AND THE DEMON KNIGHT

The moment those words almost escaped from his lips, the lock's inner workings shook against the needle's tip and sent gooseflesh across his skin.

"My fingers are shaking, so I can't muster the strength…oh! Good. It opened," she said. "Um, come in."

She opened the door slowly, revealing herself and taking Lucas's breath away. Her expression was shy, and her fluttering lashes suggested her grass-green eyes didn't know where to look. She gestured inward. Lucas nearly gasped when she gestured for him to come inside.

Her bow was so deep and refined that he nearly forgot to place his hand on his chest and return the greeting.

"Good evening, beautiful. We haven't been formally introduced. My name is Lucas Herbst. I hope you'll allow me to spend the night with you."

Starting tomorrow, he would ensure that she belonged somewhere *he* could never access her…

The woman Lucas had dreamt about waited behind the door in front of him. This had been a long, long time coming, and his hands began to sweat. He forced his hand into a fist and took a small but deep breath, preparing himself to knock on the heavy brown door.

Behind him, Finn spoke quietly. "As you requested, everything inside the room, from the furniture to the wallpaper, is new. Anna and Kate confirmed there will be no inconveniences, particularly from *him*. I've also arranged personnel to guard all the brothel's windows and doors to ensure you have no interruptions. Please call for me if you need anything else."

"Understood."

Hearing that reply, Finn mumbled under his breath. "I'm worried about that hidden knife. If too much time passes, I will return for you."

At that, he left.

Lucas took another deep breath, and once he sensed noise inside the room, he knocked.

"Y-yes?" replied the voice he'd yearned for. A hot breath left his parted lips.

"I have an appointment with you," he said. "Will you open the door?"

She hesitated briefly. "Just a moment, please."

Would she remember him? Would she remember the promise they made to meet again?

As he wondered, her hesitant voice and the faint rustling of clothes preceded the sound of her hand finding the doorknob. However, although a considerable amount of time passed, the lock didn't make the slightest click. She must've stood frozen on the other side.

Fury welled within him. He subconsciously withdrew a needle and plunged it into the keyhole.

"Cecilia, please open the door," he said. At the same time, he pressed his head against the door, willing it open.

He couldn't force it open. He had to contain himself. If she didn't open the door herself, there was no point. If she didn't offer her body to him willingly, this wouldn't amount to anything.

As much as he tried to convince himself, the needle in his grip worked the lock as if on its own.

"U-um, wait. Wait, please," she said.

He'd waited long enough. She had no idea how much he begrudged her for this. *Please*, he begged internally. *Please open the door!*

Short Story by Nekota

THE VILLAINESS AND THE DEMON KNIGHT

HICKEYS
UNFAMILIAR NIGHTGOWN
HICKEYS
BITE MARK
!!!

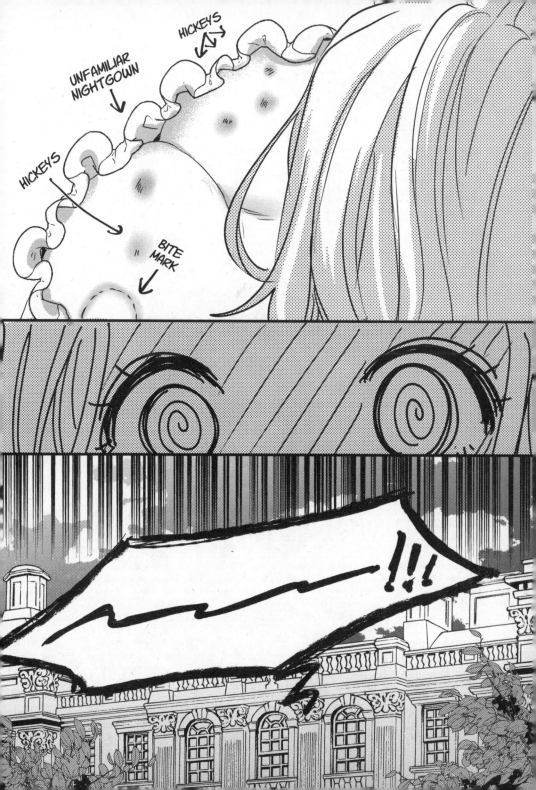

GLANCE
ちら…
HEH.
MY CHEST?
TAP
TAP

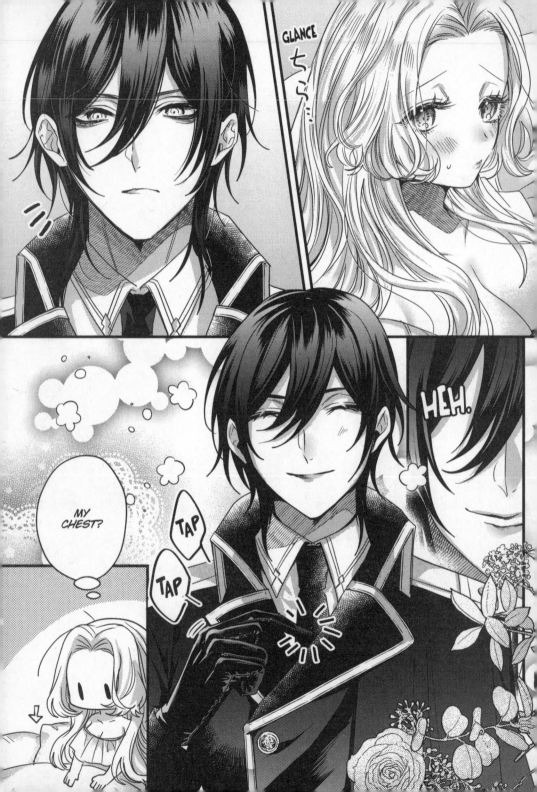

SWISH
WHAT DID HE DO LAST NIGHT?
UH...
H-HANNAH...?
EH...?

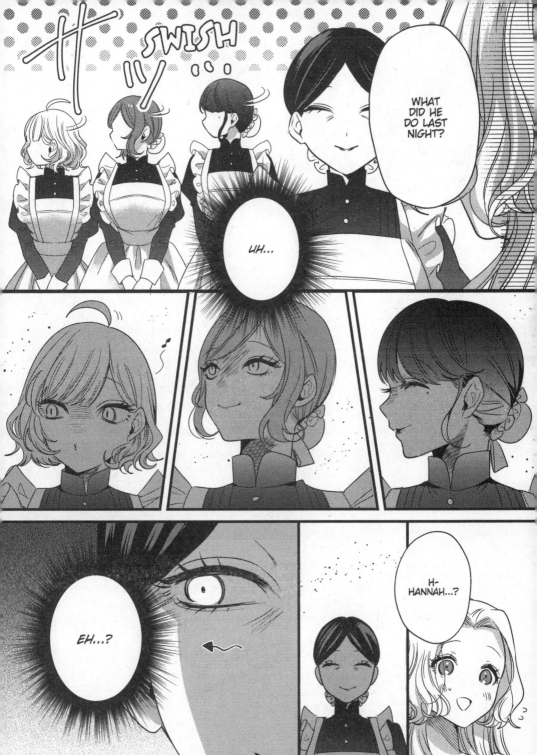

LUCAS BACKED DOWN SO EASILY.
I'M TERRIBLY SORRY FOR STARTLING YOU.
I SERVED AS LORD LUCAS'S WET NURSE, SO I'M ALLOWED TO TAKE THIS TONE WITH HIM.
THEREFORE, LADY CECILIA...
IF LORD LUCAS EVER TRIES TO FORCE YOU TO DO THINGS LIKE HE DID LAST NIGHT, DON'T HESITATE TO TELL ME.
I'LL TAKE RESPONSIBILITY AND HANDLE HIM ACCORDINGLY.
OKAY.
IT'D BE RUDE TO ATTRIBUTE HIS BEHAVIOR TO HER JUST BECAUSE SHE WAS GIVEN A PARENTAL ROLE.
HM? WAIT.

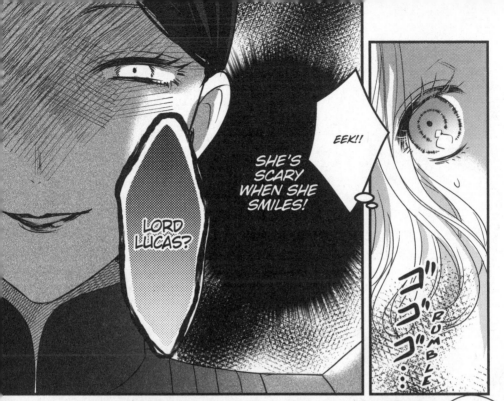

EEK!!

SHE'S SCARY WHEN SHE SMILES!

LORD LUCAS?

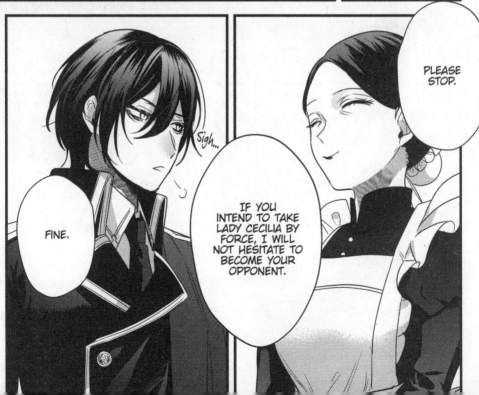

PLEASE STOP.

Sigh...

IF YOU INTEND TO TAKE LADY CECILIA BY FORCE, I WILL NOT HESITATE TO BECOME YOUR OPPONENT.

FINE.

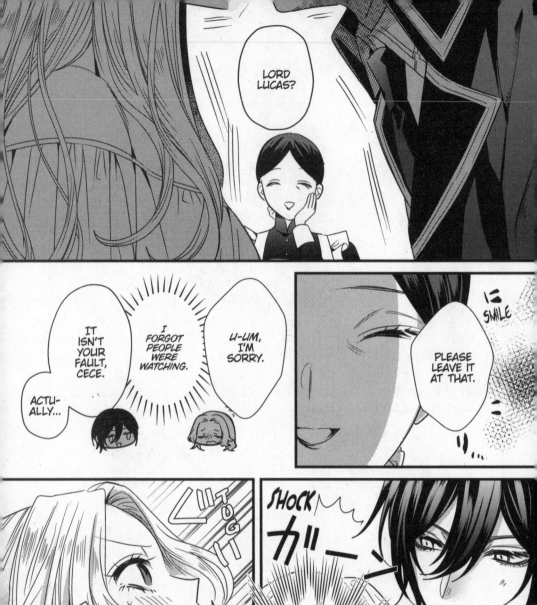

LORD LUCAS?

IT ISN'T YOUR FAULT, CECE.

ACTUALLY...

I FORGOT PEOPLE WERE WATCHING.

U-UM, I'M SORRY.

SMILE

PLEASE LEAVE IT AT THAT.

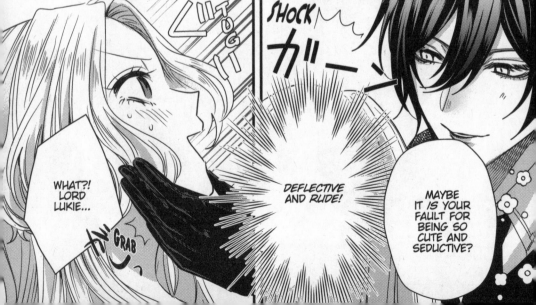

WHAT?! LORD LUKIE...

TOG

GRAB

SHOCK

DEFLECTIVE AND RUDE!

MAYBE IT *IS* YOUR FAULT FOR BEING SO CUTE AND SEDUCTIVE?

GOOD. WHAT IS IT, CECE?
STROKE
TWITCH
ARE YOU SEDUCING ME WITH THAT EXPRESSION?
EEP!
KISS
I'M NOT... MM.
AH...
HUFF.
MM...

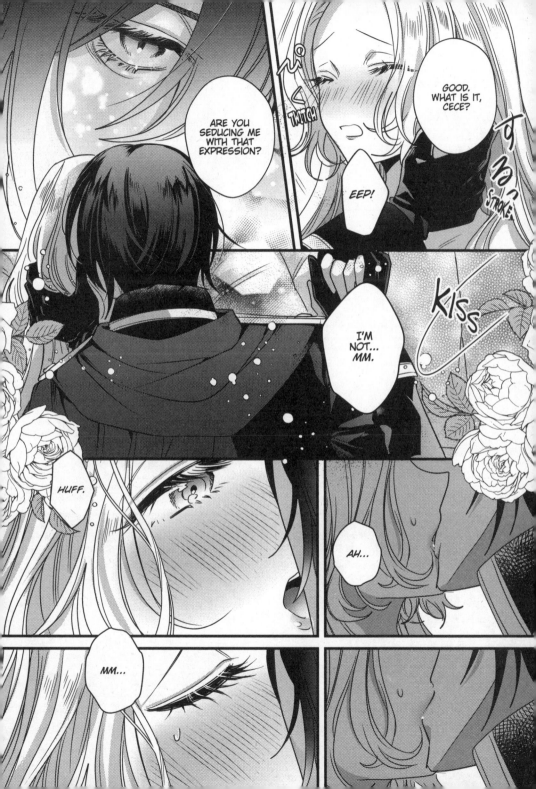

I'M GLAD.
U-UM, DUKE HERBST...
CECE.
THAT'S NOT MY NAME TO YOU, IS IT?
LORD LUKIE!
GLARE

I'M TERRIBLY SORRY FOR PUSHING YOU YOUR FIRST TIME. I WAS JUST THRILLED TO MAKE YOU MINE.
I HEARD YOU HAD A FEVER. HOW ARE YOU FEELING?
TH-THAT LOOK IS DESTRUCTIVE!
I-I'M **PERFECTLY FINE!** THANK YOU FOR YOUR CONCERN.
WAIT! "FIRST TIME"?
PUSHING ME "TOO FAR"?
WHAT IS HE SAYING IN FRONT OF OTHER PEOPLE? THIS IS SO EMBAR-RASSING!

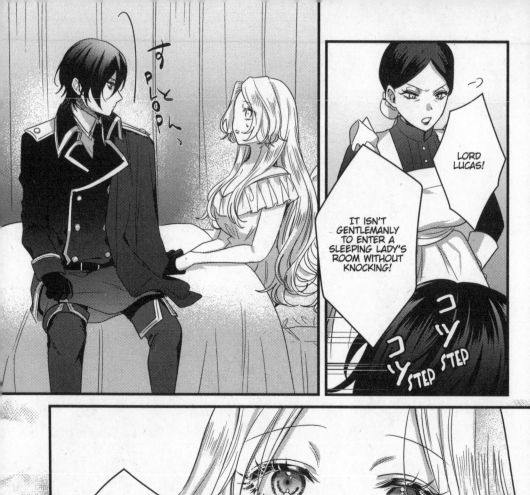

LORD LUCAS!

IT ISN'T GENTLEMANLY TO ENTER A SLEEPING LADY'S ROOM WITHOUT KNOCKING!

STEP STEP

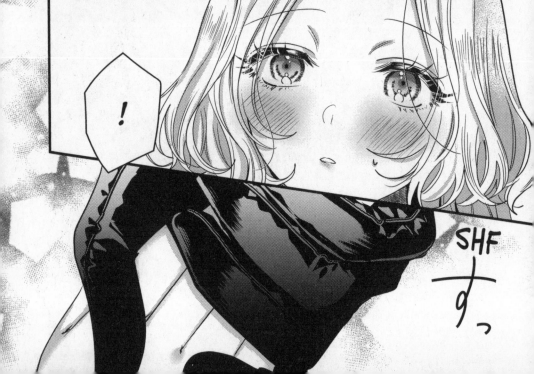

!

SHF

HE'S HERE!
GLAD TO SEE YOU AWAKE, CECE.
SMILE!

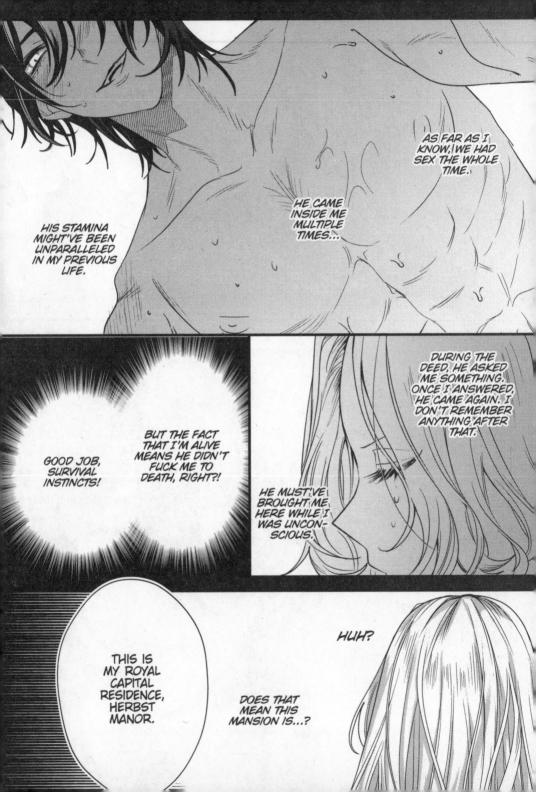

AS FAR AS I KNOW, WE HAD SEX THE WHOLE TIME.

HE CAME INSIDE ME MULTIPLE TIMES...

HIS STAMINA MIGHT'VE BEEN UNPARALLELED IN MY PREVIOUS LIFE.

DURING THE DEED, HE ASKED ME SOMETHING. ONCE I ANSWERED, HE CAME AGAIN. I DON'T REMEMBER ANYTHING AFTER THAT.

GOOD JOB, SURVIVAL INSTINCTS!

BUT THE FACT THAT I'M ALIVE MEANS HE DIDN'T FUCK ME TO DEATH, RIGHT?!

HE MUST'VE BROUGHT ME HERE WHILE I WAS UNCONSCIOUS.

HUH?

THIS IS MY ROYAL CAPITAL RESIDENCE, HERBST MANOR.

DOES THAT MEAN THIS MANSION IS...?

THEIR BOWS ARE SO POLISHED. THOSE ARE THE MANNERS OF A LADY RANKED HIGHER THAN COUNTESS!
SUCH BEAUTIFUL AND CUTE LADIES CAN SERVE AS GUARDS?
AND WHY DO I GET EXCLUSIVE ONES?
I'VE NEVER HEARD OF A PROSTITUTE WHO RECEIVED LADIES-IN-WAITING OR GUARDS.
?
WHIRL
WHAT KIND OF SITUATION HAVE I GOTTEN MYSELF INTO?
I NEED TO REMEMBER!
WHIRL

I'M HANNAH, THE HEAD MAID OF THIS MANSION.
FLUTTER
WE'VE BEEN ORDERED TO TAKE CARE OF YOU.
THIS IS ANNA...
KATE...
AND ELSA. THEY ARE YOUR EXCLUSIVE GUARDS AND LADIES-IN-WAITING.
ASK US ANYTHING YOU'D LIKE.

WH-WHAT DO I DO?!
OLD HABITS FROM MY DAYS AS A NOBLEWOMAN MADE ME SAY MY NAME!
SHE'S OBVIOUSLY A HIGH-RANKING NOBLE'S SERVANT!
I'M JUST A PROSTITUTE! AREN'T I BEING RUDE?!
SMILE
PARDON THE DELAY.

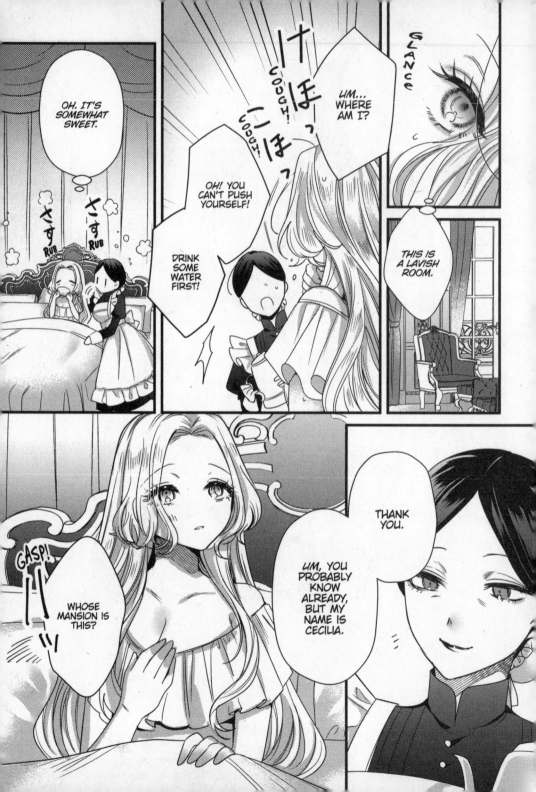

OH. IT'S SOMEWHAT SWEET.

さす RUB さす RUB

COUGH! COUGH!

OH! YOU CAN'T PUSH YOURSELF!

DRINK SOME WATER FIRST!

UM... WHERE AM I?

GLANCE

THIS IS A LAVISH ROOM.

THANK YOU.

UM, YOU PROBABLY KNOW ALREADY, BUT MY NAME IS CECILIA.

GASP!

WHOSE MANSION IS THIS?

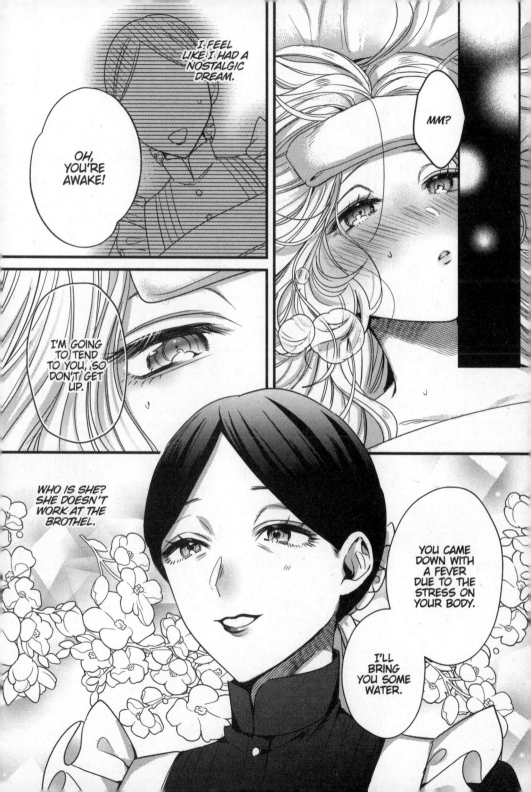

I FEEL LIKE I HAD A NOSTALGIC DREAM.

MM?

OH, YOU'RE AWAKE!

I'M GOING TO TEND TO YOU, SO DON'T GET UP.

WHO IS SHE? SHE DOESN'T WORK AT THE BROTHEL.

YOU CAME DOWN WITH A FEVER DUE TO THE STRESS ON YOUR BODY.

I'LL BRING YOU SOME WATER.

IT'S FOOLISH OF ME TO BECOME SO ABSORBED WITH HIM JUST BECAUSE HE RESEMBLES THE BOY I LOOKED UP TO.
B-DMP
ALL HE DID WAS FULFILL HIS DUTY AS AN IMPERIAL GUARD.
B-DMP
B-DMP
THAT'S WHY THIS RAPID HEARTBEAT MEANS NOTHING. YES!!
B-DMP
IT'S THE SUSPENSION BRIDGE EFFECT!!
CLATTER!
MARQUISE CECILIA?!
IT'S NOT A NOVELTY FOR A YOUNG LADY'S HEART TO RACE...
OVER SUCH A GORGEOUS, STRONG KNIGHT!!!

GASP...

--CECILIA.

MARQUISE CECILIA.

YOU LOOK PALE.

YOU SHOULD TAKE A GOOD LONG REST ONCE WE RETURN.

WERE THE MAGIC BEASTS A SHOCK TO YOUR SYSTEM?

B-DMP

THAT'S RIGHT.

B-DMP

B-DMP

Y-YES, I'LL DO THAT.

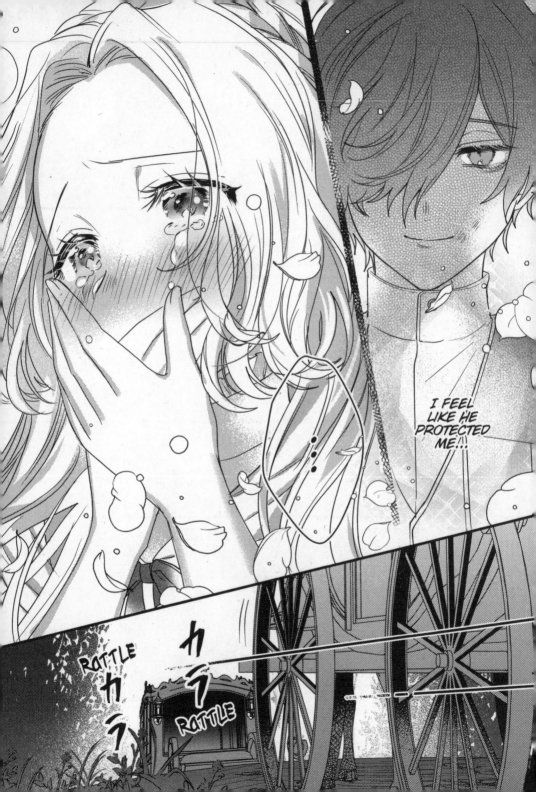

I FEEL LIKE HE PROTECTED ME...

RATTLE
カラ
カラ
カラ
RATTLE

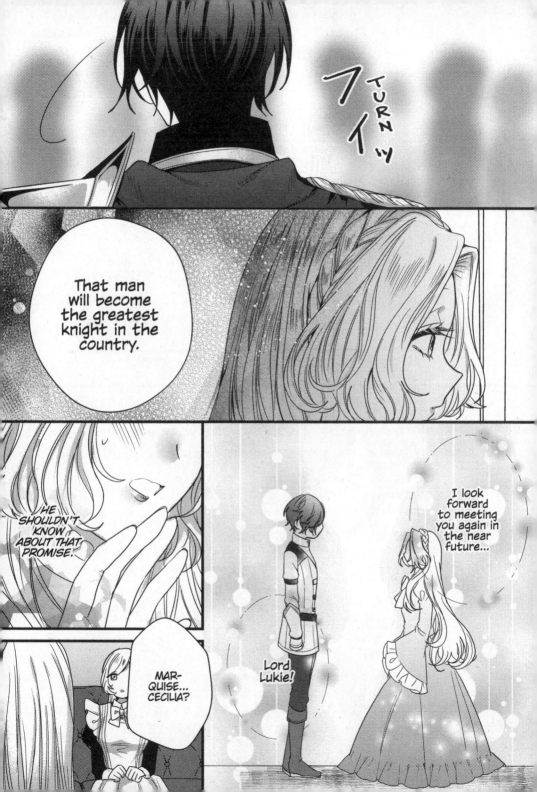

TURN

That man will become the greatest knight in the country.

HE SHOULDN'T KNOW ABOUT THAT PROMISE.

I look forward to meeting you again in the near future...

Lord Lukie!

MAR-QUISE... CECILIA?

HIS FACE WAS RATHER PLAIN, TOO...
HIS HAIR WASN'T THE COLOR OF DUSK, AND HIS EYES WEREN'T GOLD.
STILL!
!

SILENCE
Gasp
LET'S...?
LET'S GO AFTER THE REMAINING ONES!
NO... WAY...
HE CAST THEM AWAY IN A SECOND.
AND...
I KNOW THAT PROFILE...
IT WASN'T DÉJÀ VU.
I KNOW HIM.
AND THAT FEARLESS STEP.

SLASH
THUD

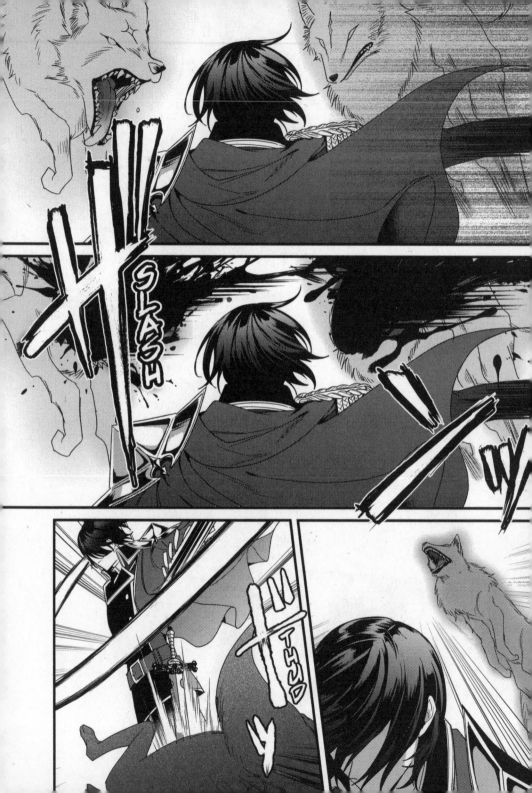

Huff...
Huff...
SCRAPE
LEAP
HERE THEY COME!
LUCAS!

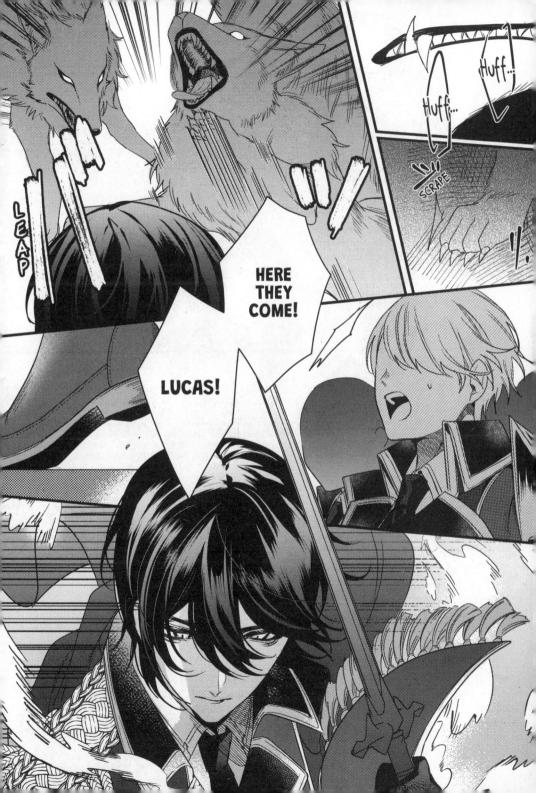

THAT HAIR COLOR!
SWISH

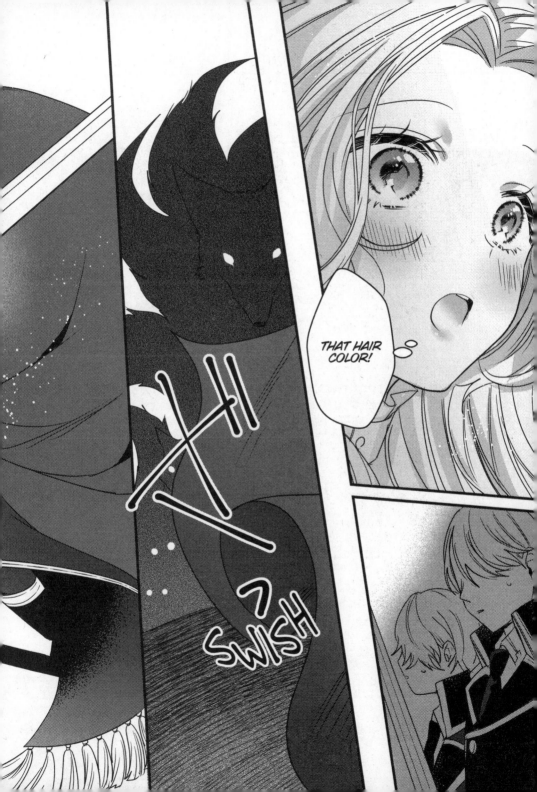

THUD
KYA!
HUH?
SST
FLASH
THIS IS A HIGH-DENSITY DEFENSE SPELL. IT'S JUST AS STRONG AS THE ONES USED TO PROTECT IMPORTANT PLACES...
SUCH AS THE THRONE ROOM.
WHO IN THE WORLD?

YOU SHOULD RUN AWAY!
I-I COULD NEVER LEAVE YOU ALL!
THE IMPERIAL ORDER DOESN'T SPECIALIZE IN COMBAT WITH MAGIC BEASTS!
WE'LL ACT AS DECOYS, SO YOU MUST GO ALONE.
I CAN'T...

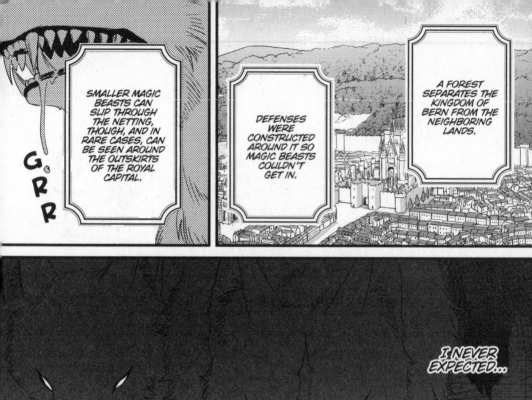

SMALLER MAGIC BEASTS CAN SLIP THROUGH THE NETTING, THOUGH, AND IN RARE CASES, CAN BE SEEN AROUND THE OUTSKIRTS OF THE ROYAL CAPITAL.

G.R.R

DEFENSES WERE CONSTRUCTED AROUND IT SO MAGIC BEASTS COULDN'T GET IN.

A FOREST SEPARATES THE KINGDOM OF BERN FROM THE NEIGHBORING LANDS.

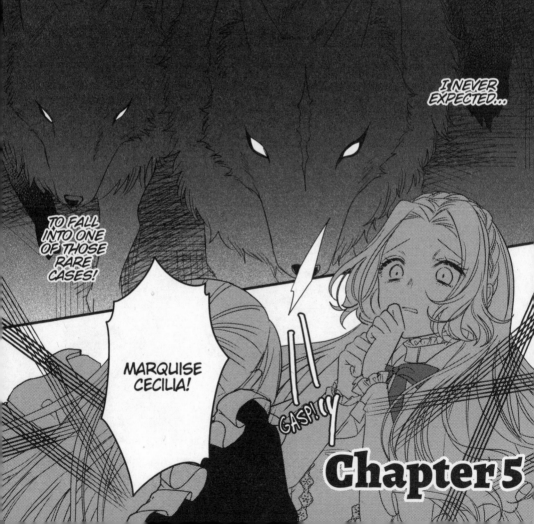

I NEVER EXPECTED...

TO FALL INTO ONE OF THOSE RARE CASES!

MARQUISE CECILIA!

GASP!

Chapter 5

THE VILLAINESS AND THE DEMON KNIGHT

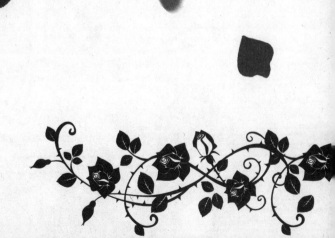

ゴ
オ
RUMBLE
オ
オ
DEMON FOXES HAVE APPEARED!
オ
オ
HOWL
オ
オ

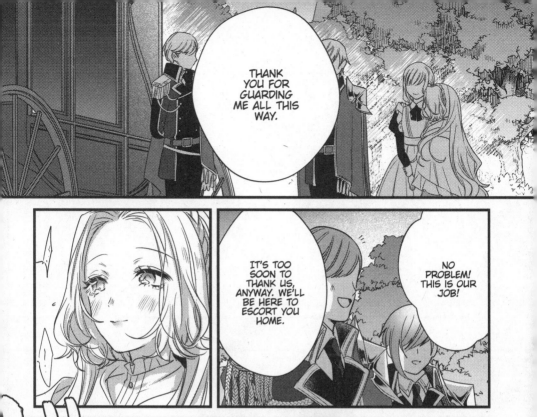

THANK YOU FOR GUARDING ME ALL THIS WAY.

IT'S TOO SOON TO THANK US, ANYWAY. WE'LL BE HERE TO ESCORT YOU HOME.

NO PROBLEM! THIS IS OUR JOB!

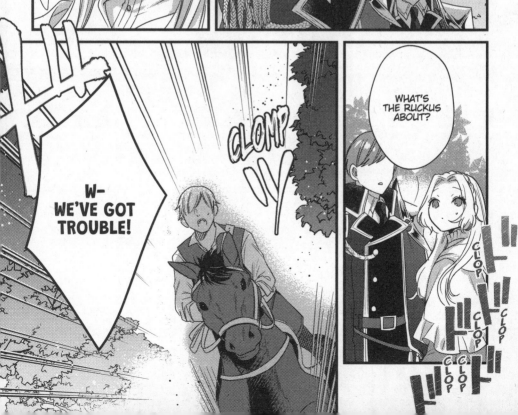

CLOMP

W-WE'VE GOT TROUBLE!

WHAT'S THE RUCKUS ABOUT?

CLOP CLOP CLOP CLOP

THE PAIN IS FADING!
THANK YOU, RAINBOW MAIDEN!
わっ
CHEER
RAINBOW...?
YOUR HEALING MAGIC IS GAINING A WONDERFUL REPUTATION!
THE MANA COMES OUT RAINBOW-COLORED AND MAKES YOU LOOK LIKE A SAINT...
OH! NO, I'M NO SAINT.
I FEEL EMBARRASSED... HAVING TWO STRANGE TITLES NOW...
BUT AS ALWAYS, PRINCE FELIX'S REPUTATION IS POOR.
I NEED TO MAKE UP FOR THAT!

AFTER THAT DAY, I ALWAYS HAD AN IMPERIAL GUARD NEARBY TO GUARD ME FOR SOME REASON.
AT THE SAME TIME, I RECEIVED PERMISSION TO SEE SICK PATIENTS.
Urgh...
I FINALLY KNOW HOW TO WIELD HEALING MAGIC.
THE ROYAL FAMILY SEEMED TO APPROVE, SO THIS KILLS TWO BIRDS WITH ONE STONE.
SHINE
OOH.
BEAUTIFUL.
SHE'S LIKE A RAINBOW MAIDEN.

WAIT FOR ME...
SQUEAK!!
MY CECILIA.
P-TMP

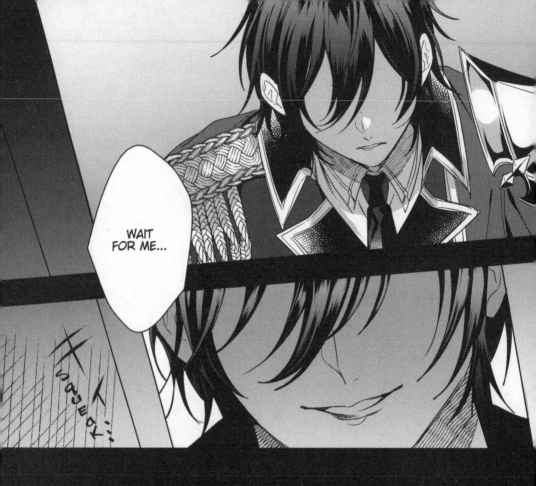

TMP
ダッ
THE GOLDEN EYES I THOUGHT I SAW BACK THEN...
RESEMBLED THAT MAN'S.
ダッ
TMP
HE LOOKED COMPLETELY DIFFERENT. HE COULDN'T POSSIBLY HAVE BEEN THE SAME PERSON...
BUT I COULDN'T HELP MY CURIOSITY.
...

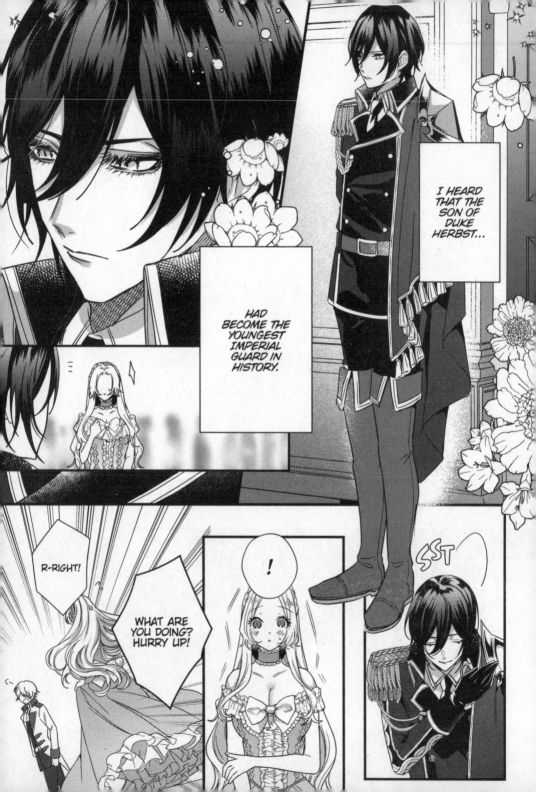

I HEARD THAT THE SON OF DUKE HERBST...

HAD BECOME THE YOUNGEST IMPERIAL GUARD IN HISTORY.

R-RIGHT!

!

WHAT ARE YOU DOING? HURRY UP!

SST

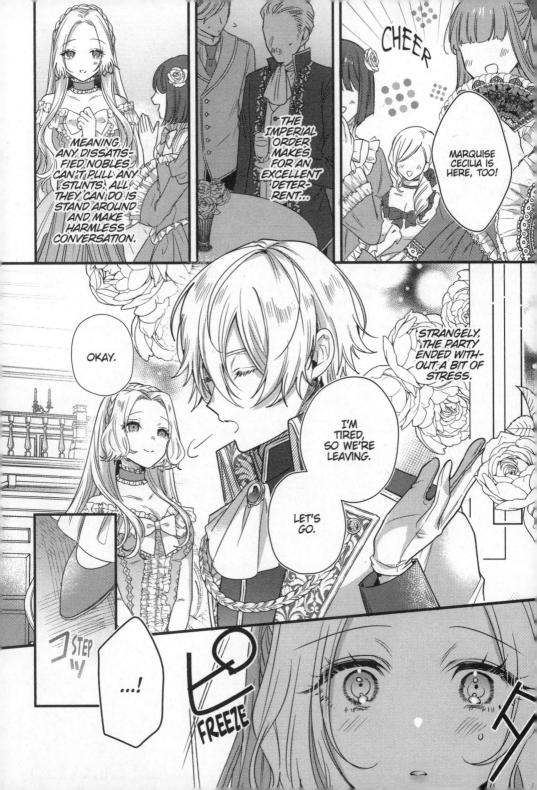

MEANING ANY DISSATISFIED NOBLES CAN'T PULL ANY STUNTS. ALL THEY CAN DO IS STAND AROUND AND MAKE HARMLESS CONVERSATION.

THE IMPERIAL ORDER MAKES FOR AN EXCELLENT DETERRENT...

CHEER

MARQUISE CECILIA IS HERE, TOO!

OKAY.

STRANGELY, THE PARTY ENDED WITHOUT A BIT OF STRESS.

I'M TIRED, SO WE'RE LEAVING.

LET'S GO.

STEP

....!

FREEZE

DON'T YOU DARE CAUSE A SCANDAL.

PRINCE FELIX?

STARE

TSK...

I HAD TO KEEP AN EYE ON PRINCE FELIX, TOO.

ALL THAT ASIDE...

GLANCE

I FEEL LIKE THERE ARE MORE KNIGHTS THAN USUAL TODAY.

All normal.

I THOUGHT THESE THINGS WERE USUALLY UNDER THE JU- RISDICTION OF THE KNIGHT OF THE BLUE ROSE.

Same here.

THE IMPERIAL ORDER IS ON DUTY TODAY?

OH! IT'S SECOND PRINCE FELIX!

MAYBE BECAUSE A PRINCE IS HERE.

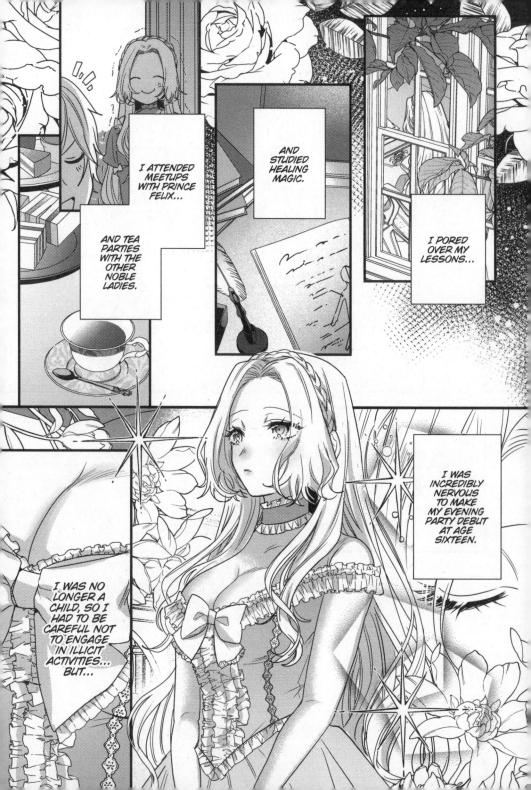

I ATTENDED MEETUPS WITH PRINCE FELIX...

AND TEA PARTIES WITH THE OTHER NOBLE LADIES.

AND STUDIED HEALING MAGIC.

I PORED OVER MY LESSONS...

I WAS INCREDIBLY NERVOUS TO MAKE MY EVENING PARTY DEBUT AT AGE SIXTEEN.

I WAS NO LONGER A CHILD, SO I HAD TO BE CAREFUL NOT TO ENGAGE IN ILLICIT ACTIVITIES... BUT...

I'M ONE, TOO.
I HOPE I'LL BECOME A CONSORT WORTHY OF YOUR PROTECTION!
I'LL TELL MY FATHER THAT I WANT TO STUDY HEALING MAGIC ONCE I RETURN HOME!
THE DAYS THAT FOLLOWED WERE TURBULENT.

WOW...
YOU'RE SUCH A HARD WORKER!
PEOPLE HAVE TO WANT TO LEARN TO GAIN THE BENEFITS.
YOU CAN'T LAMENT THAT IT'S NOT WORKING WITHOUT PUTTING IN THE EFFORT.
IF YOU GET UPSET JUST BECAUSE YOU'VE BEEN MADE TO CARRY A SMALL BURDEN...
YOU CAN'T LOOK THE PEOPLE YOU'RE MEANT TO SUPPORT IN THE EYE!

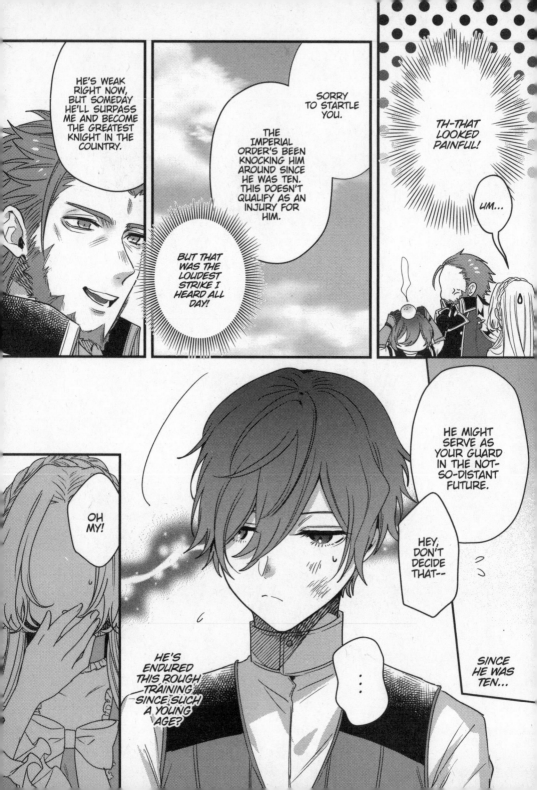

HE'S WEAK RIGHT NOW, BUT SOMEDAY HE'LL SURPASS ME AND BECOME THE GREATEST KNIGHT IN THE COUNTRY.

SORRY TO STARTLE YOU.

THE IMPERIAL ORDER'S BEEN KNOCKING HIM AROUND SINCE HE WAS TEN. THIS DOESN'T QUALIFY AS AN INJURY FOR HIM.

BUT THAT WAS THE LOUDEST STRIKE I HEARD ALL DAY!

TH-THAT LOOKED PAINFUL!

UM...

HE MIGHT SERVE AS YOUR GUARD IN THE NOT-SO-DISTANT FUTURE.

HEY, DON'T DECIDE THAT--

OH MY!

HE'S ENDURED THIS ROUGH TRAINING SINCE SUCH A YOUNG AGE?

SINCE HE WAS TEN...

I KNOW ALL ABOUT HIS IDENTITY, THOUGH!

MEMBERS OF THE ROYAL FAMILY USE SHAPESHIFTING MAGIC DURING TRAINING WITH THE IMPERIAL ORDER TO ENSURE NO ONE FUSSES OVER THEIR IDENTITY OR CUTS CORNERS...

HENCE THE INFORMALITY OF HIS NICKNAME, LUKIE.

BEING WATCHED FLUSTERED ME SO MUCH THAT I NEARLY DROPPED THE SHAPESHIFTING SPELL ON MY EYES!

MEANWHILE, LUCAS WAS PANICKING INTERNALLY.

※Inner thoughts

※AT THIS POINT, HIS EMOTIONS HADN'T BEEN FULLY REALIZED YET.

I MADE HER WORRY. NOW SHE'S GOING TO THINK I'M WEAK AND FEEL ANXIOUS ABOUT ME. GOD, THAT'S EMBARRASSING.

UH...

YEAH...

EXCUSE ME! IS YOUR HAND ALL RIGHT?

THWACK

?!

FLINCH

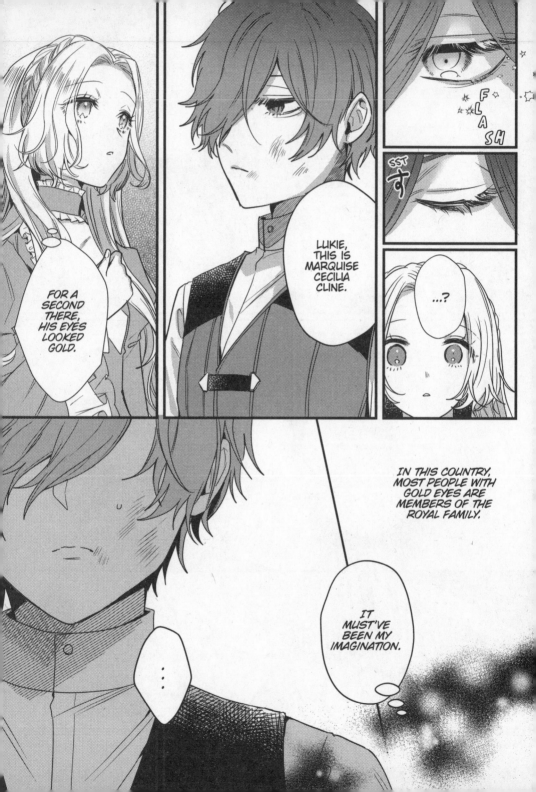

FOR A SECOND THERE, HIS EYES LOOKED GOLD.

LUKIE, THIS IS MARQUISE CECILIA CLINE.

...?

FLASH

SST すっ

IN THIS COUNTRY, MOST PEOPLE WITH GOLD EYES ARE MEMBERS OF THE ROYAL FAMILY.

IT MUST'VE BEEN MY IMAGINATION.

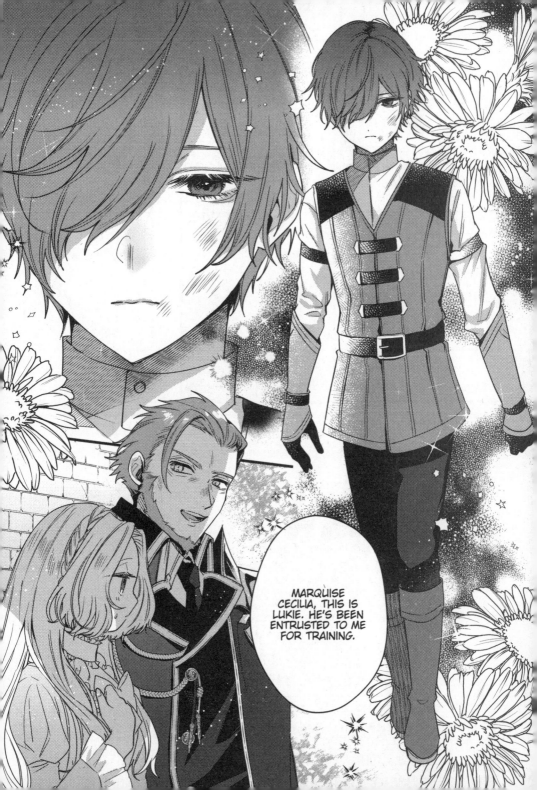

MARQUISE CECILIA, THIS IS LUKIE. HE'S BEEN ENTRUSTED TO ME FOR TRAINING.

THAT'S ENOUGH!
FLEX
FLEX
...
Argh! Damn it!
IS HIS HAND INJURED?
HE NEEDS TREAT-MENT.
GRIP
I CAN'T USE HEALING MAGIC.
I... I WANT TO BECOME SOMEONE WHO CAN HEAL HIS WOUNDS...
HEY, LUKIE! COME HERE!

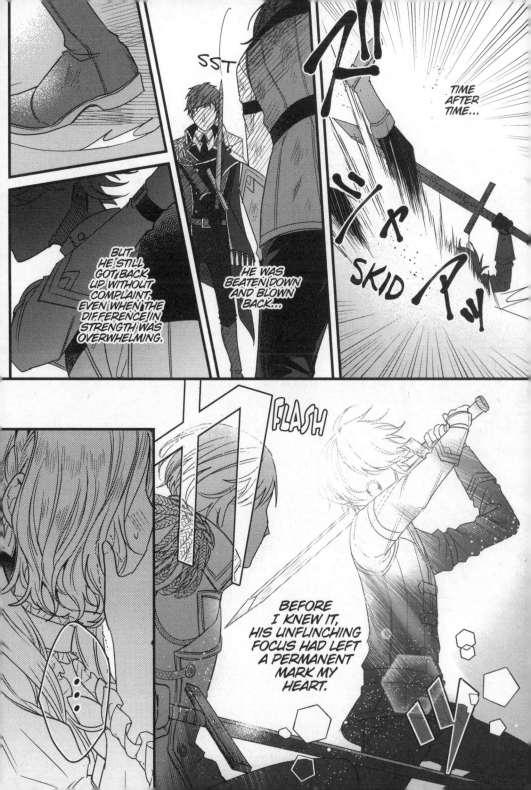

TIME AFTER TIME...

SST

All

KR

SKID

FWA

BUT HE STILL GOT BACK UP, WITHOUT COMPLAINT, EVEN WHEN THE DIFFERENCE IN STRENGTH WAS OVERWHELMING.

HE WAS BEATEN DOWN AND BLOWN BACK...

FLASH

BEFORE I KNEW IT, HIS UNFLINCHING FOCUS HAD LEFT A PERMANENT MARK MY HEART.

THERE HE IS.
CLACK
...!
CLACK
CLACK
CLACK
CLACK

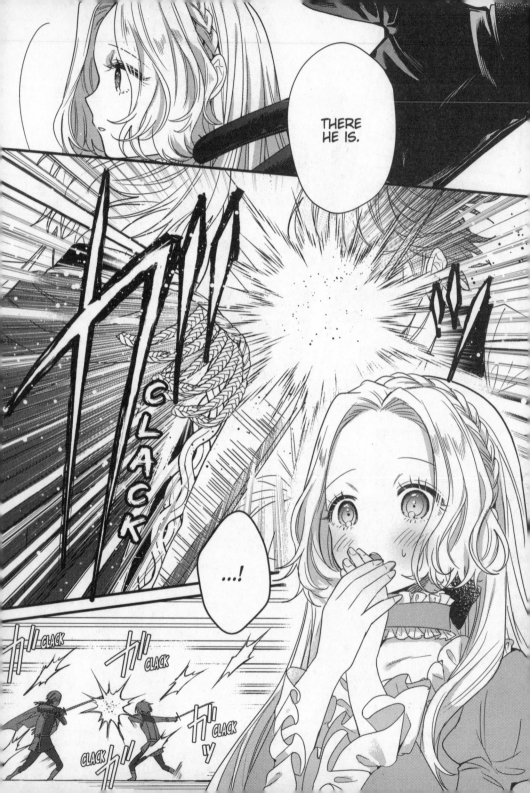

WOW, YOU'RE GLUM TODAY!

NOW THAT I WAS THE SECOND PRINCE'S FIANCÉE...

VICE-CAPTAIN OF THE IMPERIAL GUARD ANDREAS WEBBER CAME TO INTRODUCE MY GUARD.

LORD ANDREAS! AT LEAST KNOCK!

AH HA HA! SORRY 'BOUT THAT.

GAH HA HA!!

ONE OF THEM ISN'T AN OFFICIAL GUARD YET, BUT HE'S OF SIMILAR AGE TO MARQUISE CECILIA.

WE'VE GOT A PROMISING BUNCH OF NEW RECRUITS THIS YEAR.

IT'S BRIGHT OUT.

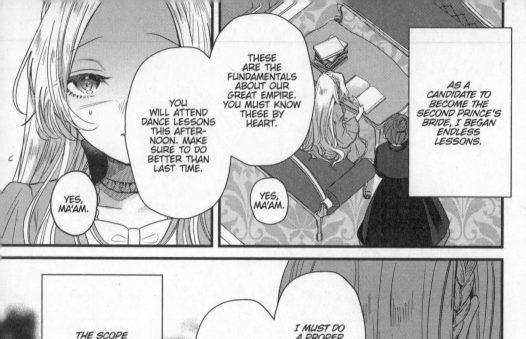

YOU WILL ATTEND DANCE LESSONS THIS AFTER-NOON. MAKE SURE TO DO BETTER THAN LAST TIME.

THESE ARE THE FUNDAMENTALS ABOUT OUR GREAT EMPIRE. YOU MUST KNOW THESE BY HEART.

AS A CANDIDATE TO BECOME THE SECOND PRINCE'S BRIDE, I BEGAN ENDLESS LESSONS.

YES, MA'AM.

YES, MA'AM.

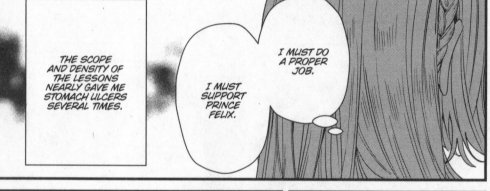

THE SCOPE AND DENSITY OF THE LESSONS NEARLY GAVE ME STOMACH ULCERS SEVERAL TIMES.

I MUST SUPPORT PRINCE FELIX.

I MUST DO A PROPER JOB.

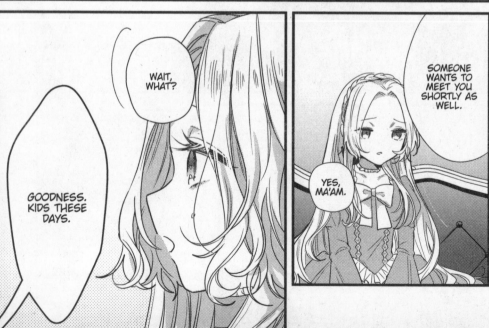

WAIT, WHAT?

GOODNESS. KIDS THESE DAYS.

SOMEONE WANTS TO MEET YOU SHORTLY AS WELL.

YES, MA'AM.

I HAVE TO MAKE UP FOR ALL OF HIS FAULTS.
CLENCH
ギュッ
I MUST DO A PROPER JOB.
AFTER THAT DAY, MY VIVID LIFE GREW DULL.
IT FELT LIKE I HAD SHACKLES AROUND MY ANKLES.

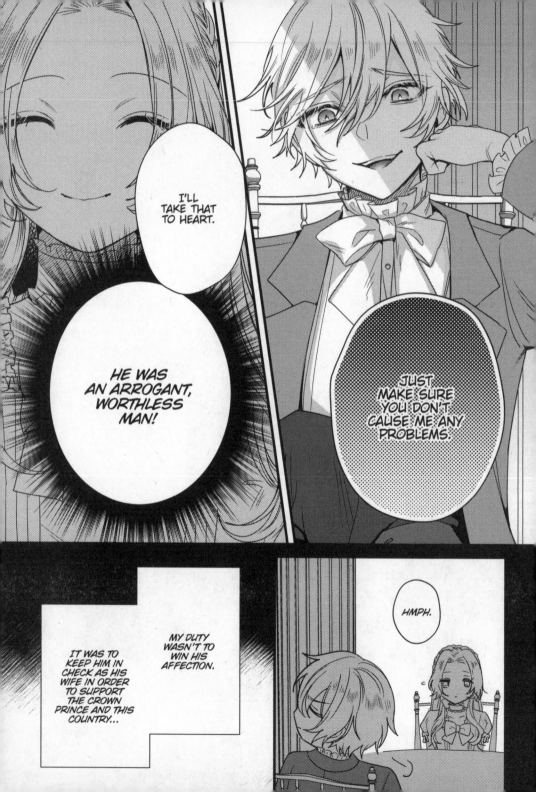

I'LL TAKE THAT TO HEART.

HE WAS AN ARROGANT, WORTHLESS MAN!

JUST MAKE SURE YOU DON'T CAUSE ME ANY PROBLEMS.

MY DUTY WASN'T TO WIN HIS AFFECTION.

IT WAS TO KEEP HIM IN CHECK AS HIS WIFE IN ORDER TO SUPPORT THE CROWN PRINCE AND THIS COUNTRY...

HMPH.

UM...
JUST BECAUSE I'M FROM THE ROYAL FAMILY...
Sigh... はぁ…
DOESN'T MEAN I SHOULDN'T BE ALLOWED TO HAVE INPUT ON MY FIANCÉE.
YOUR FACE IS FINE, BUT YOU'RE PLAIN.
YOU LOOK UPTIGHT AND FLAT.
YOUR MOTHER HAD A MORE WOMANLY BODY.
WHEN I FIRST MET PRINCE FELIX...
WELL, I GUESS YOU WOULDN'T BE LIKE THAT AT YOUR AGE.

Chapter 4

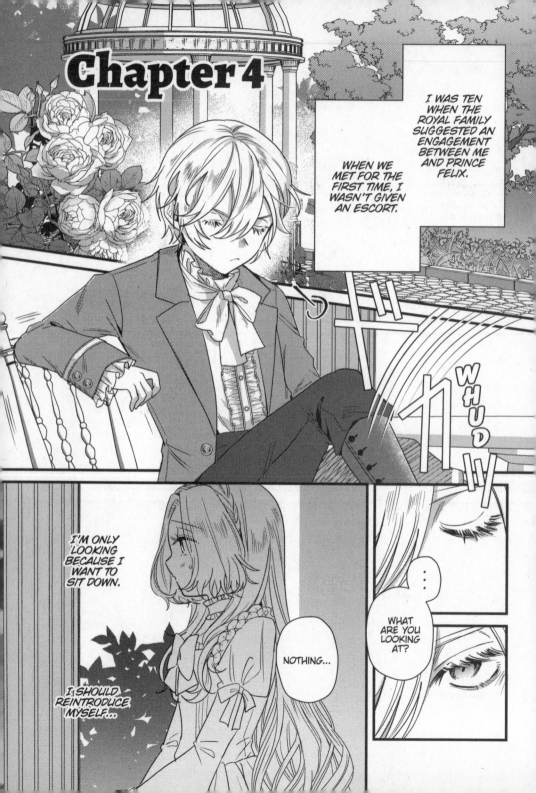

I WAS TEN WHEN THE ROYAL FAMILY SUGGESTED AN ENGAGEMENT BETWEEN ME AND PRINCE FELIX.

WHEN WE MET FOR THE FIRST TIME, I WASN'T GIVEN AN ESCORT.

WHUD

I'M ONLY LOOKING BECAUSE I WANT TO SIT DOWN.

I SHOULD REINTRODUCE MYSELF...

NOTHING...

WHAT ARE YOU LOOKING AT?

...

THE VILLAINESS AND THE DEMON KNIGHT

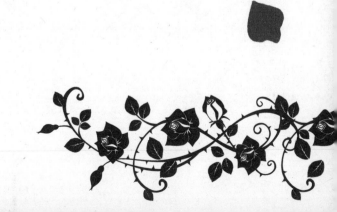

ふ〜
ゆっ
FLUTTER
HEH HEH.

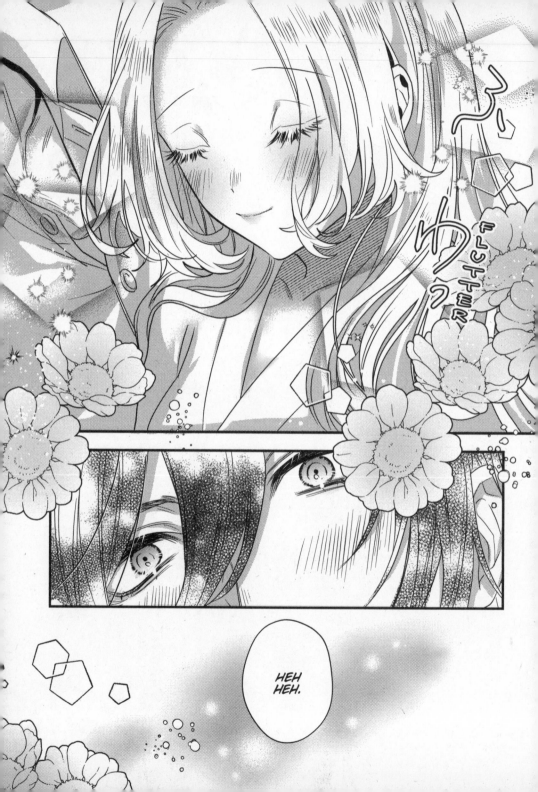

MM...

SHE'S TOO LIGHT.

CECE?

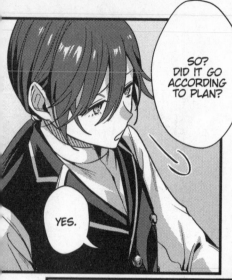

SO?
DID IT GO
ACCORDING
TO PLAN?

YES.

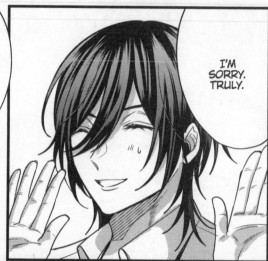

I'M
SORRY.
TRULY.

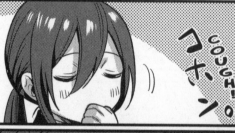

WELL
THEN, I
SHALL WAIT
FOR YOU
DOWNSTAIRS
WITH THE
OTHERS.

COUGH!

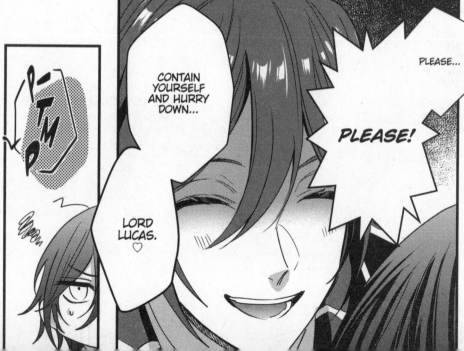

PLEASE...

PLEASE!

CONTAIN
YOURSELF
AND HURRY
DOWN...

P-T-M-P

LORD
LUCAS. ♡

CLANG!
WHOOSH
Tak
WHY?!
WHY WOULD YOU WASTE A DAGGER OF THE HIGHEST QUALITY AND DURABILITY, WHICH YOU *JUST* GOT, ON THIS?!
I DIDN'T BUY THAT SO YOU COULD PIN A DRESS TO THE WALL!
WHAT DID YOU COME TO THIS BROTHEL FOR, ANYWAY?!
...

LORD LUCAS, I BROUGHT YOU A CHANGE OF CLOTHES.
WHERE'S HANNAH AND THE OTHERS?
THEY JUST ARRIVED AT THE BROTHEL.
EVERYTHING IS SETTLED WITH THE MISTRESS, SO I IMAGINE THEY ARE WAITING AT THE ENTRANCE ON STANDBY.
GOODNESS, WHAT A MESS YOU'VE MADE.
てきぱき
BRISK BRISK
DRESS
......
AH.
SORRY.

I NEVER EXPECTED MIA TO DEMAND HE SEND YOU TO A BROTHEL.
YOU NEVER KNOW WHAT HIDES BENEATH A WOMAN'S APPEARANCE.
YOU WERE FORCED INTO THIS, CECE.
KNOCK
KNOCK
FINN?
STEP
PARDON MY INTRUSION.

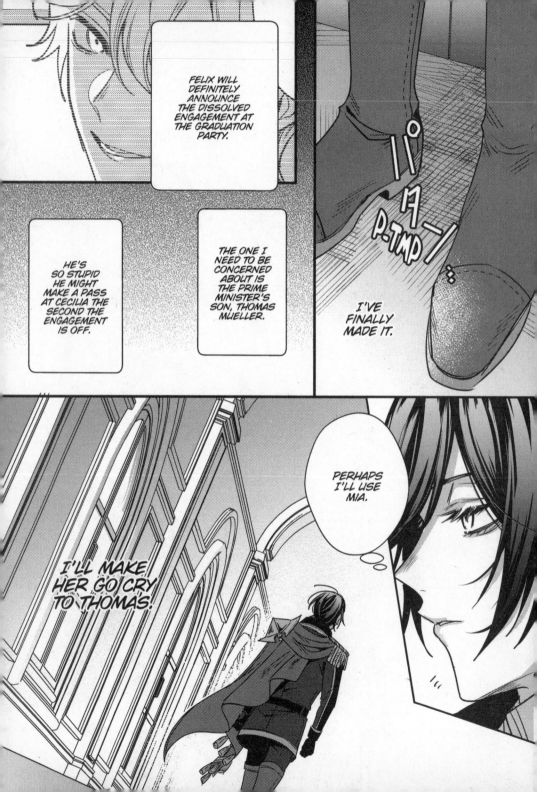

FELIX WILL DEFINITELY ANNOUNCE THE DISSOLVED ENGAGEMENT AT THE GRADUATION PARTY.

HE'S SO STUPID HE MIGHT MAKE A PASS AT CECILIA THE SECOND THE ENGAGEMENT IS OFF.

THE ONE I NEED TO BE CONCERNED ABOUT IS THE PRIME MINISTER'S SON, THOMAS MUELLER.

P-TMP

I'VE FINALLY MADE IT.

PERHAPS I'LL USE MIA.

I'LL MAKE HER GO CRY TO THOMAS!

IF YOU WAIT A BIT LONGER, YOU'RE DUE TO INHERIT MARSHAL WEBBER'S HERO'S CREST AND ECKESACHS, AREN'T YOU?
ONLY ONE PERSON CAN WIELD ECKESACHS.
AND THE KINGDOM CAN'T IGNORE ANY WISH FROM THAT PERSON.
THEY CAN REQUEST GIFTS AND REWARDS.
Eck achs
A "GIFT"?
A-ALL I DID WAS SUGGEST A MEANS OF HAVING HER!
YOU JUST CALLED HER A *GIFT*.
YANK
FINE, I GET IT!
JUST PUT A LID ON YOUR BLOODLUST!

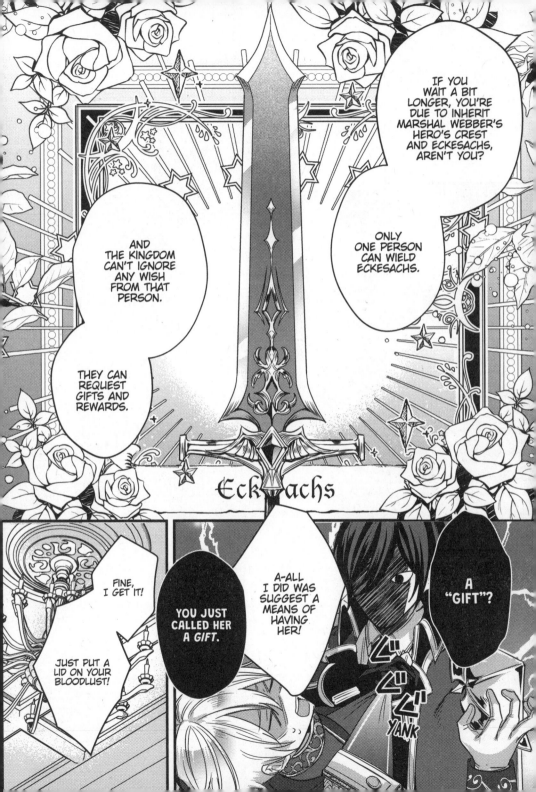

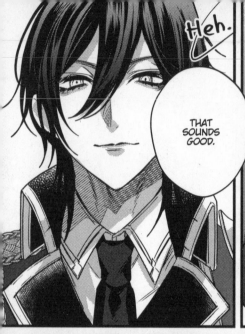

Heh.

THAT SOUNDS GOOD.

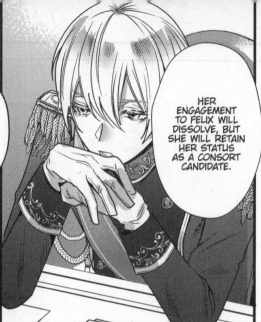

HER ENGAGEMENT TO FELIX WILL DISSOLVE, BUT SHE WILL RETAIN HER STATUS AS A CONSORT CANDIDATE.

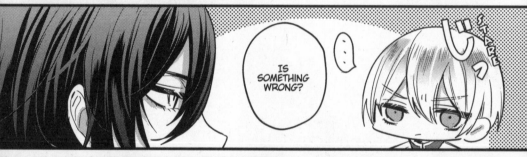

...

IS SOMETHING WRONG?

STARE

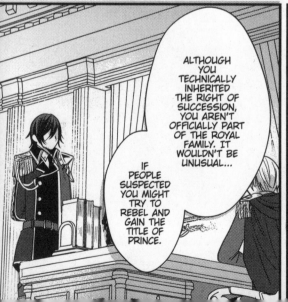

ALTHOUGH YOU TECHNICALLY INHERITED THE RIGHT OF SUCCESSION, YOU AREN'T OFFICIALLY PART OF THE ROYAL FAMILY. IT WOULDN'T BE UNUSUAL...

IF PEOPLE SUSPECTED YOU MIGHT TRY TO REBEL AND GAIN THE TITLE OF PRINCE.

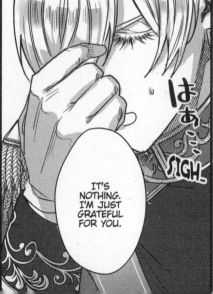

SIGH.

IT'S NOTHING. I'M JUST GRATEFUL FOR YOU.

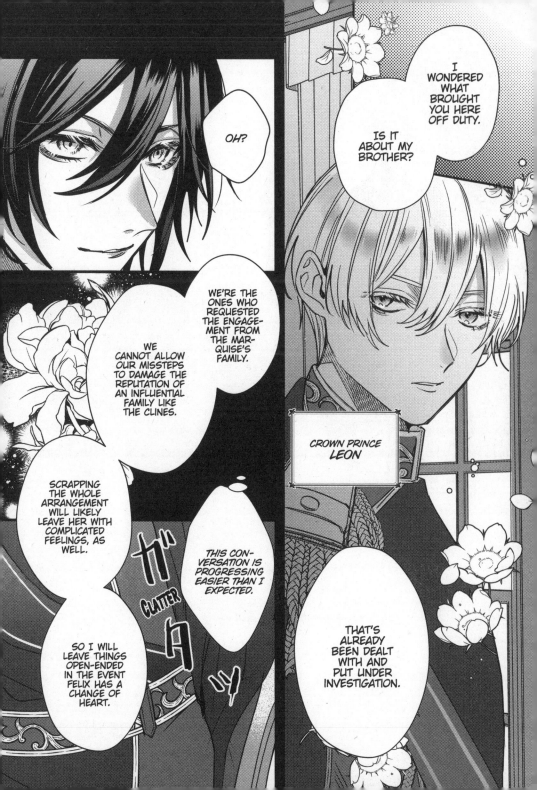

OH?

I WONDERED WHAT BROUGHT YOU HERE OFF DUTY.

IS IT ABOUT MY BROTHER?

WE'RE THE ONES WHO REQUESTED THE ENGAGEMENT FROM THE MARQUISE'S FAMILY.

WE CANNOT ALLOW OUR MISSTEPS TO DAMAGE THE REPUTATION OF AN INFLUENTIAL FAMILY LIKE THE CLINES.

CROWN PRINCE LEON

SCRAPPING THE WHOLE ARRANGEMENT WILL LIKELY LEAVE HER WITH COMPLICATED FEELINGS, AS WELL.

THIS CONVERSATION IS PROGRESSING EASIER THAN I EXPECTED.

CLATTER

SO I WILL LEAVE THINGS OPEN-ENDED IN THE EVENT FELIX HAS A CHANGE OF HEART.

THAT'S ALREADY BEEN DEALT WITH AND PUT UNDER INVESTIGATION.

CLENCH
AFTER MUCH ADMONISHING, I CONVINCED HIM TO CUT HER OFF, TOO.
OKAY. I'LL TALK TO MY FATHER.
THANK YOU.
ADOLF AND HIS PARENTS SWALLOWED THEIR TEARS AND MADE A DECISION.
ALL THAT'S LEFT IS THE ROYAL FAMILY.
ENTER.

IT WORKS IN MY FAVOR IF MIA AND FELIX GROW INTIMATE...

HAA...

WHAT WILL BEFALL MY FAMILY?

THEY'LL END UP HORRIBLY DESTITUTE.

BUT FOR ADOLF AND THE REST OF THE COUNT'S FAMILY...

AND ROPED ADOLF INTO MY PLAN.

ADOLF.

I CUT OFF MIA, USED MY INFLUENCE AS A HERBST TO KEEP THE FAULT OFF THE REST OF THE MEYER FAMILY...

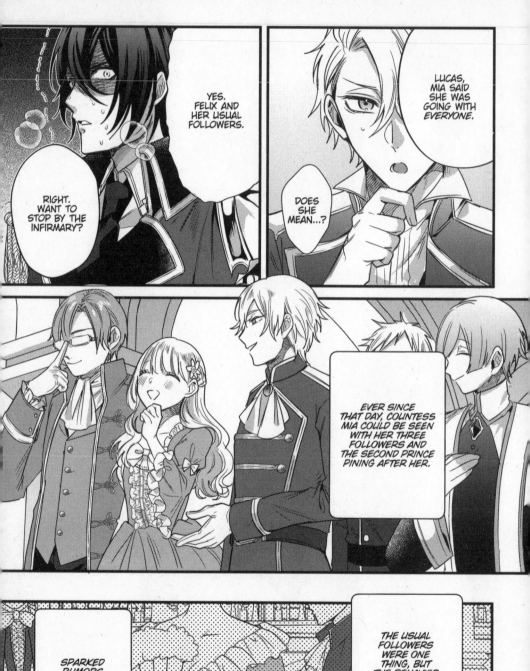

YES. FELIX AND HER USUAL FOLLOWERS.

RIGHT. WANT TO STOP BY THE INFIRMARY?

LUCAS, MIA SAID SHE WAS GOING WITH EVERYONE.

DOES SHE MEAN...?

EVER SINCE THAT DAY, COUNTESS MIA COULD BE SEEN WITH HER THREE FOLLOWERS AND THE SECOND PRINCE PINING AFTER HER.

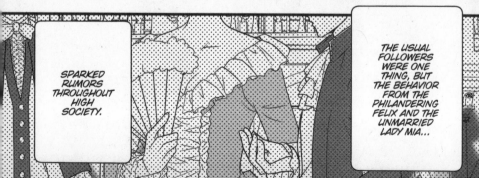

SPARKED RUMORS THROUGHOUT HIGH SOCIETY.

THE USUAL FOLLOWERS WERE ONE THING, BUT THE BEHAVIOR FROM THE PHILANDERING FELIX AND THE UNMARRIED LADY MIA...

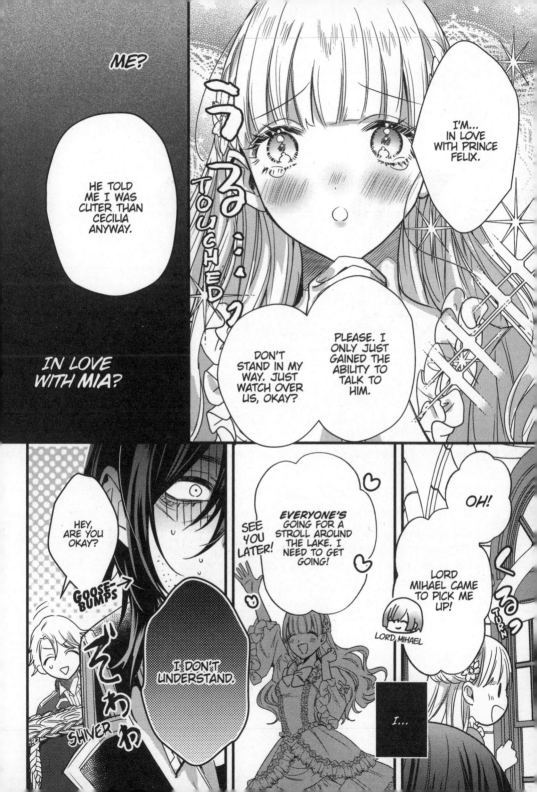

ME?

HE TOLD ME I WAS CUTER THAN CECILIA ANYWAY.

I'M... IN LOVE WITH PRINCE FELIX.

こつるこつる TOUCHED?

IN LOVE WITH MIA?

DON'T STAND IN MY WAY. JUST WATCH OVER US, OKAY?

PLEASE. I ONLY JUST GAINED THE ABILITY TO TALK TO HIM.

HEY, ARE YOU OKAY?

GOOSE-BUMPS →

ぞわわ SHIVER

I DON'T UNDERSTAND.

SEE YOU LATER!

EVERYONE'S GOING FOR A STROLL AROUND THE LAKE. I NEED TO GET GOING!

OH!

LORD MIHAEL CAME TO PICK ME UP!

LORD MIHAEL

I...

I BELIEVE YOU ARE AWARE...
BUT HE ALREADY HAS A FIANCÉE.
DON'T YOU UNDERSTAND HOW IT LOOKS LIKE WHEN A LOWER-STATUS, UNMARRIED WOMAN IS CLOSE TO HIM?
LORD LUCAS...
GIGGLE
くすっ
GIGGLE
くすっ
HEH HEH HEH.
ARE YOU JEALOUS?
I LOVE YOU, LORD LUCAS, BUT ONLY AS A BROTHER.
WHAT?

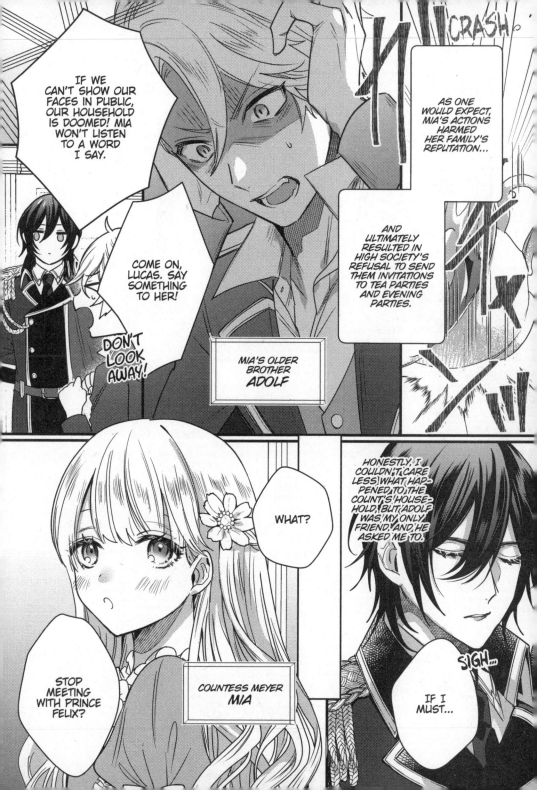

IF WE CAN'T SHOW OUR FACES IN PUBLIC, OUR HOUSEHOLD IS DOOMED! MIA WON'T LISTEN TO A WORD I SAY.

AS ONE WOULD EXPECT, MIA'S ACTIONS HARMED HER FAMILY'S REPUTATION...

CRASH

COME ON, LUCAS. SAY SOMETHING TO HER!

DON'T LOOK AWAY!

AND ULTIMATELY RESULTED IN HIGH SOCIETY'S REFUSAL TO SEND THEM INVITATIONS TO TEA PARTIES AND EVENING PARTIES.

MIA'S OLDER BROTHER ADOLF

HONESTLY, I COULDN'T CARE LESS WHAT HAPPENED TO THE COUNT'S HOUSEHOLD, BUT ADOLF WAS MY ONLY FRIEND, AND HE ASKED ME TO.

WHAT?

SIGH...

STOP MEETING WITH PRINCE FELIX?

COUNTESS MEYER MIA

IF I MUST...

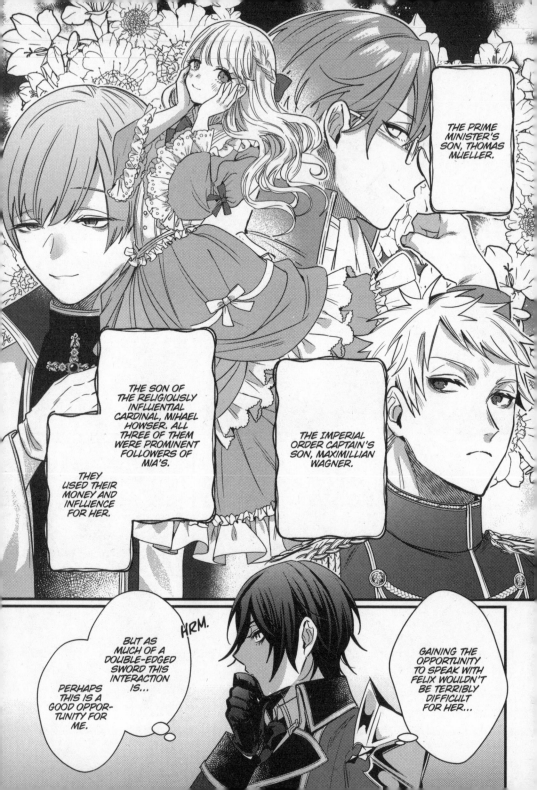

THE PRIME MINISTER'S SON, THOMAS MUELLER.

THE SON OF THE RELIGIOUSLY INFLUENTIAL CARDINAL, MIHAEL HOWSER. ALL THREE OF THEM WERE PROMINENT FOLLOWERS OF MIA'S.

THE IMPERIAL ORDER CAPTAIN'S SON, MAXIMILLIAN WAGNER.

THEY USED THEIR MONEY AND INFLUENCE FOR HER.

HRM.

BUT AS MUCH OF A DOUBLE-EDGED SWORD THIS INTERACTION IS...

PERHAPS THIS IS A GOOD OPPORTUNITY FOR ME.

GAINING THE OPPORTUNITY TO SPEAK WITH FELIX WOULDN'T BE TERRIBLY DIFFICULT FOR HER...

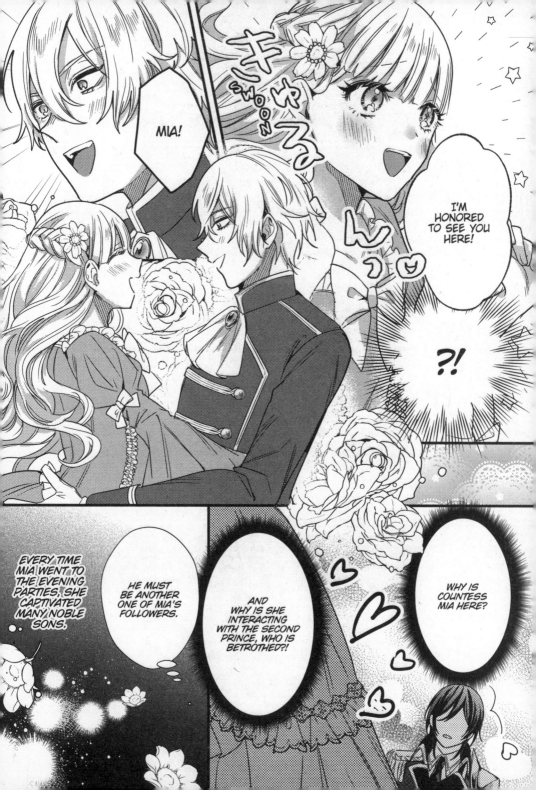

MIA!

きゅるるる
SWOON

I'M HONORED TO SEE YOU HERE!

?!

EVERY TIME MIA WENT TO THE EVENING PARTIES, SHE CAPTIVATED MANY NOBLE SONS.

HE MUST BE ANOTHER ONE OF MIA'S FOLLOWERS.

AND WHY IS SHE INTERACTING WITH THE SECOND PRINCE, WHO IS BETROTHED?!

WHY IS COUNTESS MIA HERE?

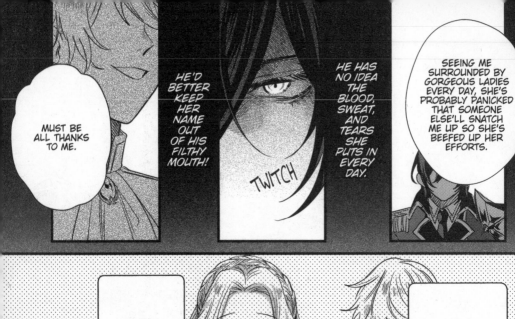

MUST BE ALL THANKS TO ME.

HE'D BETTER KEEP HER NAME OUT OF HIS FILTHY MOUTH!

TWITCH

HE HAS NO IDEA THE BLOOD, SWEAT, AND TEARS SHE PUTS IN EVERY DAY.

SEEING ME SURROUNDED BY GORGEOUS LADIES EVERY DAY, SHE'S PROBABLY PANICKED THAT SOMEONE ELSE'LL SNATCH ME UP SO SHE'S BEEFED UP HER EFFORTS.

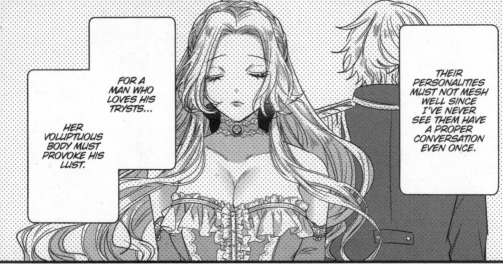

FOR A MAN WHO LOVES HIS TRYSTS...

HER VOLUPTUOUS BODY MUST PROVOKE HIS LUST.

THEIR PERSONALITIES MUST NOT MESH WELL SINCE I'VE NEVER SEE THEM HAVE A PROPER CONVERSATION EVEN ONCE.

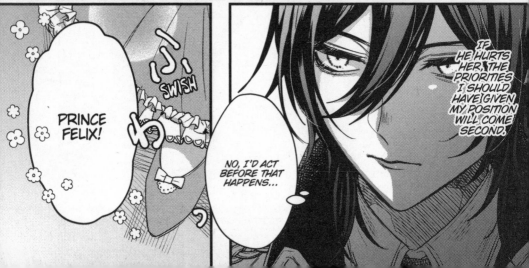

PRINCE FELIX!

SWISH

NO, I'D ACT BEFORE THAT HAPPENS...

IF HE HURTS HER, THE PRIORITIES I SHOULD HAVE GIVEN MY POSITION WILL COME SECOND.

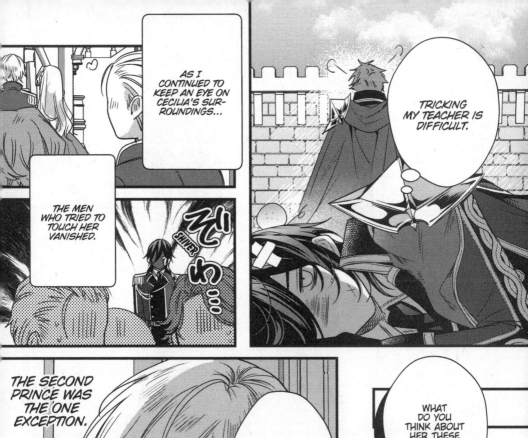

AS I CONTINUED TO KEEP AN EYE ON CECILIA'S SURROUNDINGS...

TRICKING MY TEACHER IS DIFFICULT.

THE MEN WHO TRIED TO TOUCH HER VANISHED.

SHIVER

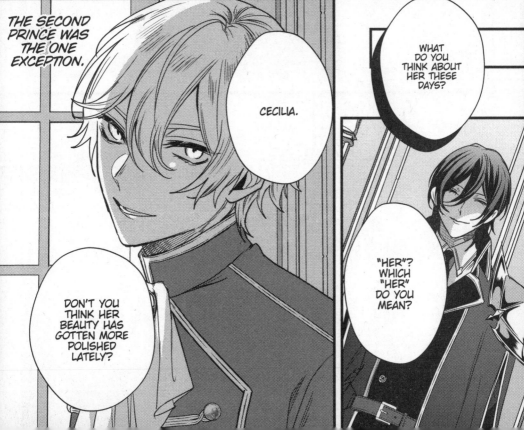

THE SECOND PRINCE WAS THE ONE EXCEPTION.

CECILIA.

WHAT DO YOU THINK ABOUT HER THESE DAYS?

DON'T YOU THINK HER BEAUTY HAS GOTTEN MORE POLISHED LATELY?

"HER"? WHICH "HER" DO YOU MEAN?

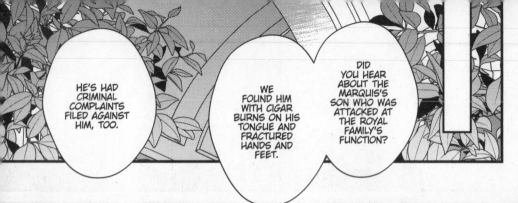

HE'S HAD CRIMINAL COMPLAINTS FILED AGAINST HIM, TOO.

WE FOUND HIM WITH CIGAR BURNS ON HIS TONGUE AND FRACTURED HANDS AND FEET.

DID YOU HEAR ABOUT THE MARQUIS'S SON WHO WAS ATTACKED AT THE ROYAL FAMILY'S FUNCTION?

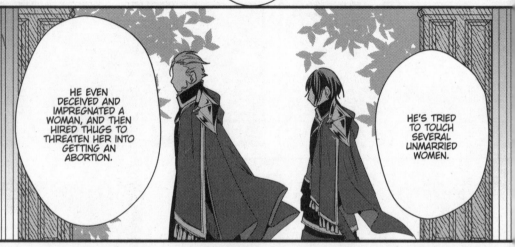

HE EVEN DECEIVED AND IMPREGNATED A WOMAN, AND THEN HIRED THUGS TO THREATEN HER INTO GETTING AN ABORTION.

HE'S TRIED TO TOUCH SEVERAL UNMARRIED WOMEN.

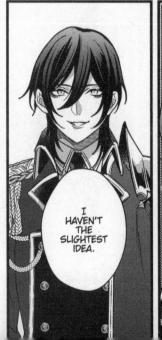

I HAVEN'T THE SLIGHTEST IDEA.

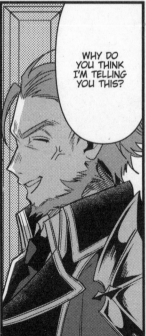

WHY DO YOU THINK I'M TELLING YOU THIS?

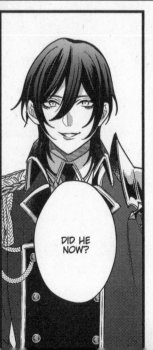

DID HE NOW?

Sob
Sob
WHY IS THIS HAPPENING TO ME?
SHE'S JUST A CONSORT CANDIDATE!
CECILIA...
DOES HE MEAN...
MY CECILIA?
"JUST"...
A CONSORT CANDIDATE?

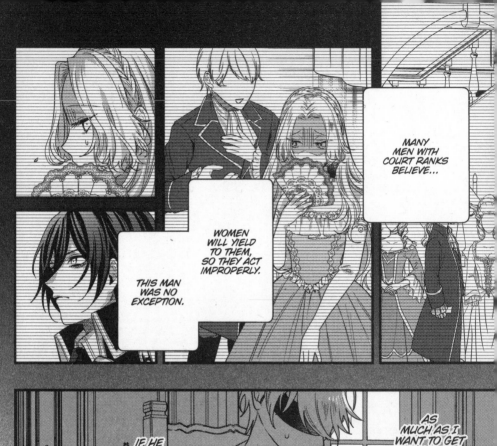

MANY MEN WITH COURT RANKS BELIEVE...

WOMEN WILL YIELD TO THEM, SO THEY ACT IMPROPERLY.

THIS MAN WAS NO EXCEPTION.

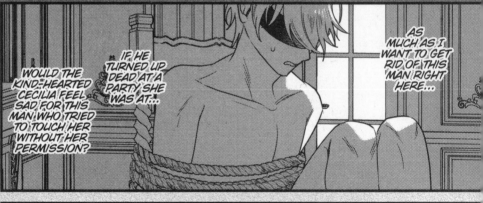

WOULD THE KIND-HEARTED CECILIA FEEL SAD FOR THIS MAN WHO TRIED TO TOUCH HER WITHOUT HER PERMISSION?

IF HE TURNED UP DEAD AT A PARTY SHE WAS AT...

AS MUCH AS I WANT TO GET RID OF THIS MAN RIGHT HERE...

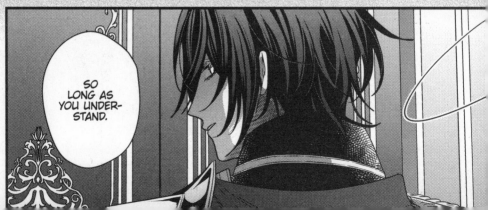

SO LONG AS YOU UNDER-STAND.

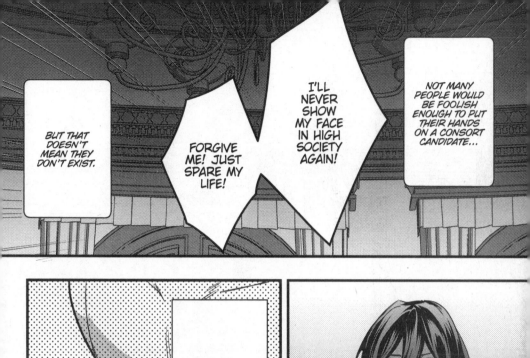

BUT THAT DOESN'T MEAN THEY DON'T EXIST.

FORGIVE ME! JUST SPARE MY LIFE!

I'LL NEVER SHOW MY FACE IN HIGH SOCIETY AGAIN!

NOT MANY PEOPLE WOULD BE FOOLISH ENOUGH TO PUT THEIR HANDS ON A CONSORT CANDIDATE...

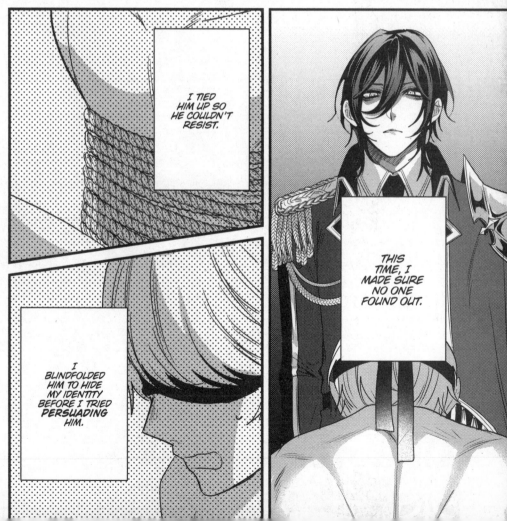

I TIED HIM UP SO HE COULDN'T RESIST.

THIS TIME, I MADE SURE NO ONE FOUND OUT.

I BLINDFOLDED HIM TO HIDE MY IDENTITY BEFORE I TRIED PERSUADING HIM.

Chapter 3

FOR SOME REASON, ANDREAS WAS FURIOUS.
SHOUT
DAMMIT, LUKIE!
YOU WENT...
SURPRISE!
TOO FAR!!
WHAM
THE NEXT WEEK OF TRAINING MADE ME FEEL LIKE I WAS GOING TO DIE.
NEXT TIME I'LL ACT MORE CALMLY.
THAT WAY, I WON'T GET CAUGHT!

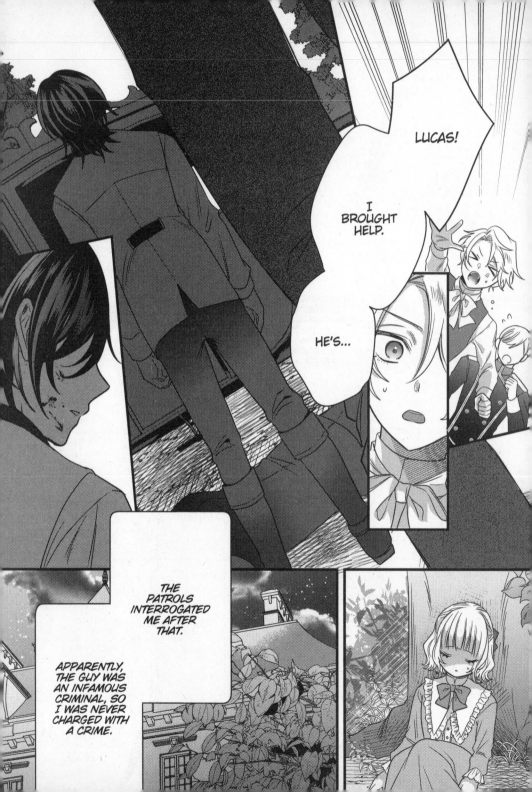

LUCAS!

I BROUGHT HELP.

HE'S...

THE PATROLS INTERROGATED ME AFTER THAT.

APPARENTLY, THE GUY WAS AN INFAMOUS CRIMINAL, SO I WAS NEVER CHARGED WITH A CRIME.

BA-
DUMP

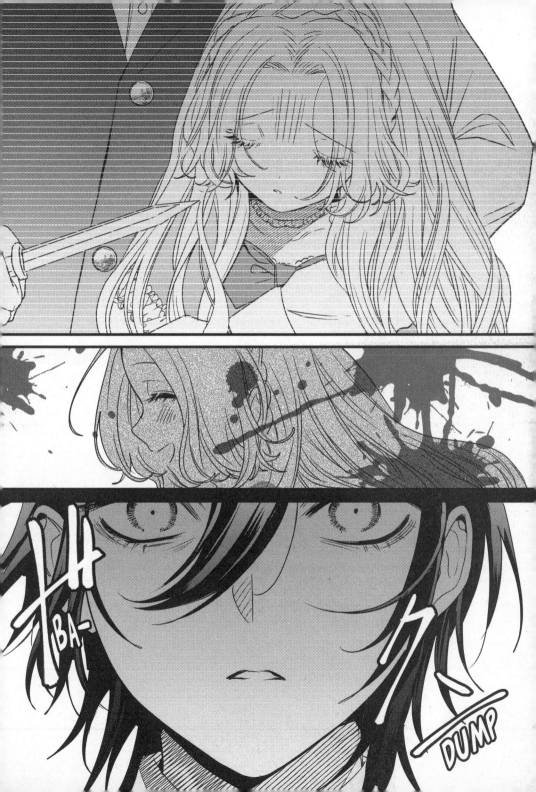

THE SECOND THIS GUY STEPS DOWN FROM THE CARRIAGE, I'LL CLOSE THE GAP.
L-LISTEN HERE. DON'T YOU DARE MOVE...
THIS IS A GOOD CHANCE TO TEST ALL THE STRENGTH AND SKILLS I'VE LEARNED.
FWOOP
SPARKLE
SHP
Lord Lukie!

THEY'RE LAUGHABLY WRONG.
I'D NEVER LET CECILIA'S WOULD-BE KIDNAPPERS GET AWAY.
EVEN SO, I CAN'T TOUCH THEM. MIA'S IN THE WAY.
I HAVE TO ACCEPT...
FINE.
はぁ…
SIGH...

LET HER GO.
EEK...
ST-STAY BACK!
WE WERE ASKED TO GET THE GIRL WITH THE AMBER HAIR!
Y-YOU CAN HAVE THIS ONE BACK UNHARMED.
JUST GET AWAY FROM OUR CARRIAGE!
THEY THINK I'LL LET THEM GO SIMPLY FOR HANDING MIA BACK UNHARMED?

THIS GIRL WOULD FETCH A GOOD PRICE, TOO.
TONS OF PERVERTS WOULD LOVE TO *TRAIN* A NOBLE GIRL.
B-DMP
B-DMP
B-DMP
AMBER?
B-DMP
?!
CLATTER
WHAT'S GOING ON?! DID OUR PURSUERS--?!
FWIP
SMACK

A FEW MONTHS LATER, MY CHILDHOOD FRIEND MIA, COUNT MEYER'S DAUGHTER, WAS KIDNAPPED.
SETTLE DOWN!
KYAAAAA!
BIG BROTHER!
GET HER OUTTA HERE!
ADOLF! CALL FOR THE NEAREST PATROL KNIGHT!
DASH
OKAY!
MOST KIDS WOULD JUST RUN AWAY FROM DANGEROUS ADULTS.
DAMMIT, YOU SNATCHED THE WRONG GIRL!
SORRY, OKAY?!
I NEED TO BUY TIME UNTIL HELP ARRIVES...
WHAT?
ARE THEY ARGUING?
WE WERE TOLD TO GRAB THE GIRL WITH THE AMBER HAIR!

THEN I
COULD HAVE
HER.

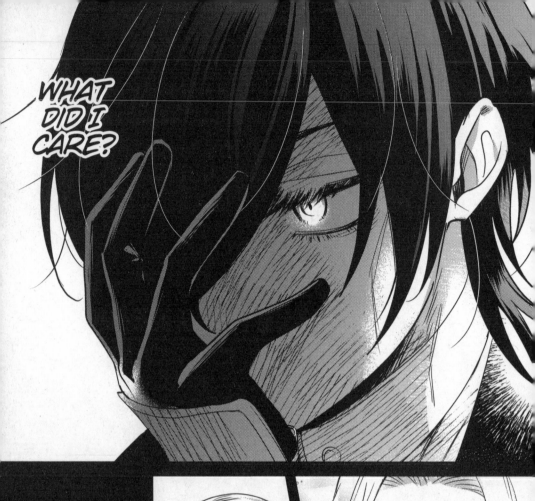

WHAT DID I CARE?

IF THE RIGHT OF SUCCESSION WASN'T ENOUGH TO HAVE HER...

I JUST NEEDED TO BECOME A PRINCE, DIDN'T I?

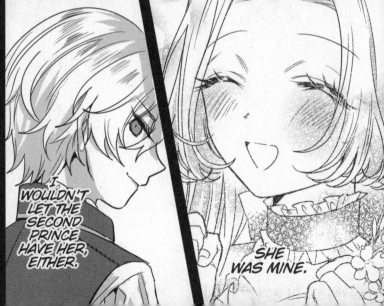

I WOULDN'T LET THE SECOND PRINCE HAVE HER, EITHER.

SHE WAS MINE.

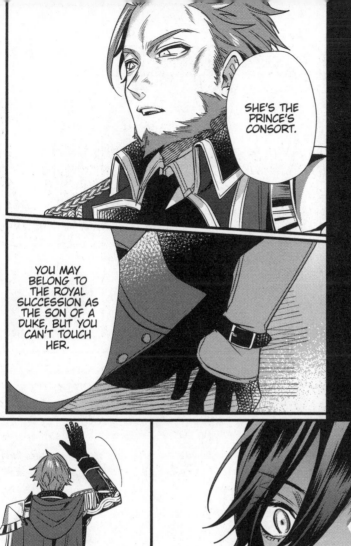

SHE'S THE PRINCE'S CONSORT.

THAT'S NOT GOOD, LUCAS.

YOU MAY BELONG TO THE ROYAL SUCCESSION AS THE SON OF A DUKE, BUT YOU CAN'T TOUCH HER.

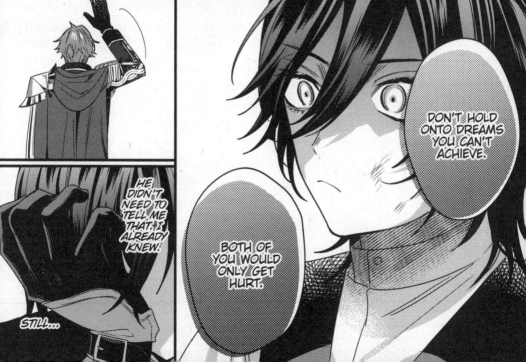

DON'T HOLD ONTO DREAMS YOU CAN'T ACHIEVE.

HE DIDN'T NEED TO TELL ME THAT. I ALREADY KNEW!

BOTH OF YOU WOULD ONLY GET HURT.

STILL...

わい
BUSTLE
わい
BUSTLE
Nice, Lukie!
Wow, Vice-Captain!
NGH...
THUD
HEY, NOW. YOU ALWAYS GET BACK UP NO MATTER HOW MANY TIMES YOU FALL.
KU KU KU!
YOU DIDN'T LIKE BEING KNOCKED ON YOUR BUTT IN FRONT OF LADY CLINE?
!
FLINCH
BULLSEYE, HUH?
すん…
SULK
You just flinched!

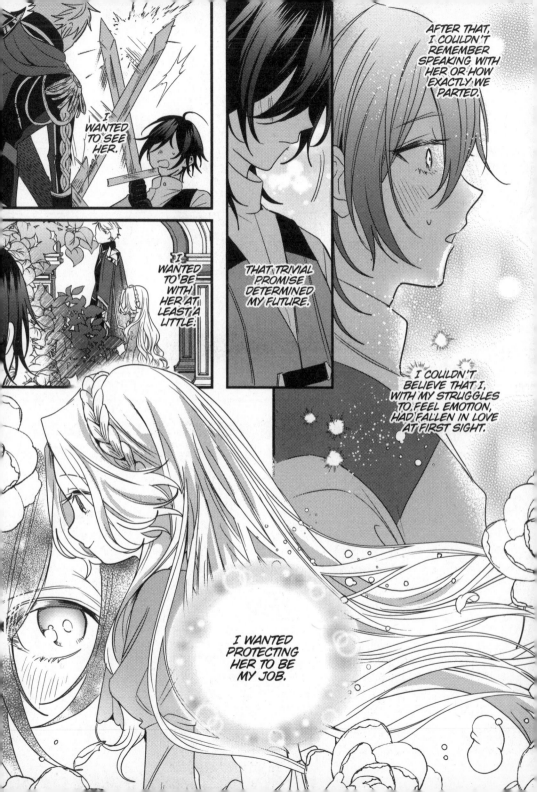

I WANTED TO SEE HER.

I WANTED TO BE WITH HER AT LEAST A LITTLE.

AFTER THAT, I COULDN'T REMEMBER SPEAKING WITH HER OR HOW EXACTLY WE PARTED.

THAT TRIVIAL PROMISE DETERMINED MY FUTURE.

I COULDN'T BELIEVE THAT I, WITH MY STRUGGLES TO FEEL EMOTION, HAD FALLEN IN LOVE AT FIRST SIGHT.

I WANTED PROTECTING HER TO BE MY JOB.

キラ SPARKLE
YOU'RE SUCH A HARD WORKER!
キラ SPARKLE
I'M WORRIED ABOUT FULFILLING MY DUTIES AS THE PRINCE'S CONSORT, BUT...
NOTHING CAN BE ACHIEVED WITHOUT EFFORT!
I HOPE I'LL BECOME A CONSORT WORTHY OF YOUR PROTECTION!
MMPH!
I LOOK FORWARD TO MEETING YOU AGAIN IN THE NEAR FUTURE...
LORD LUKIE!

ACT DIGNIFIED!
...!
HAHAHAHA!
THE IMPERIAL ORDER'S BEEN KNOCKING HIM AROUND SINCE HE WAS TEN. THIS DOESN'T QUALIFY AS AN INJURY FOR HIM.
Ruffle
HE'S WEAK RIGHT NOW, BUT SOMEDAY HE'LL SURPASS ME AND BECOME THE GREATEST KNIGHT IN THE COUNTRY.
HE MIGHT SERVE AS YOUR GUARD IN THE NOT-SO-DISTANT FUTURE.
HEY, DON'T DECIDE THAT--
OH MY!

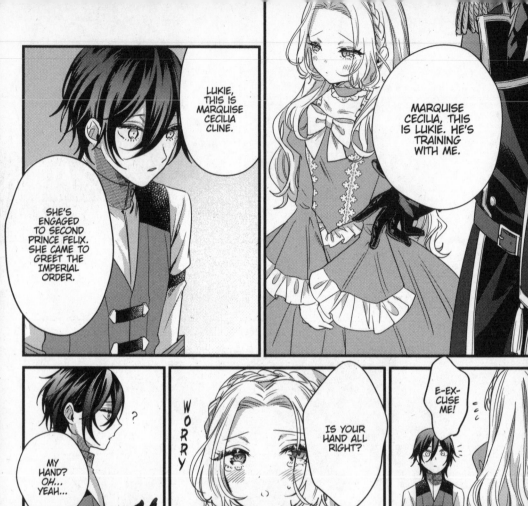

LUKIE, THIS IS MARQUISE CECILIA CLINE.

MARQUISE CECILIA, THIS IS LUKIE. HE'S TRAINING WITH ME.

SHE'S ENGAGED TO SECOND PRINCE FELIX. SHE CAME TO GREET THE IMPERIAL ORDER.

MY HAND? OH... YEAH...

WORRY

IS YOUR HAND ALL RIGHT?

E-EX-CUSE ME!

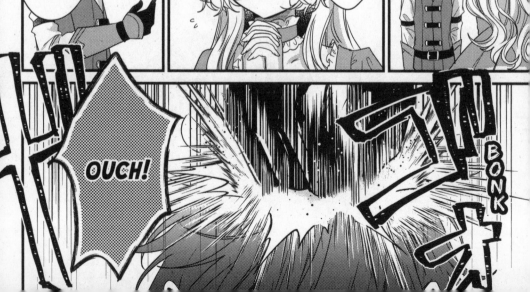

OUCH!

BONK

CLANG
FROM THE BOTTOM, HUH?
BUT...
YOU'RE STILL TOO WEAK!
FINISH!
CLACK
AWW MAN! I WANTED A WHACK AT HIM!
IT DIDN'T MATTER WHETHER THE MATCH WAS BETWEEN AN ADULT AND A CHILD.
NO MATTER HOW VAST THE DIFFERENCE OF STAMINA AND MUSCLE STRENGTH...
IF I COULDN'T KEEP A GRIP ON MY SWORD, DEATH AWAITED ME.
I NEED TO TRAIN MORE.
GRIP
HEY, LUKIE! COME HERE!
MORE PUSH-UPS AS PUNISH-MENT?

YOU LACK A FOUNDATION OF STRENGTH!
GO TO THAT CORNER AND DO EIGHT HUNDRED SIT-UPS AND PUSH-UPS EACH!
...!
AT ANY RATE, THE IMPERIAL GUARD'S TRAINING REGIMEN WAS HELL ON MY TEN-YEAR-OLD BODY.
Begin!
CLACK
WHEN I WAS THIRTEEN, AROUND THE TIME MY BODY GREW ACCUSTOMED TO TRAINING...
WHOOSH
IF I KEEP THIS UP, I'LL GET STUCK ON DEFENSE.
HOW AM I SUPPOSED TO BEAT AN ADULT WHO'S STRONGER AND BIGGER THAN I AM?
TMP
DASH

WHEN I WAS TEN, MY FATHER ASKED THE KING FOR A FAVOR...
AND HAD THE VICE-CAPTAIN OF THE IMPERIAL GUARD COME TEACH ME.
YO!
WHY THE GLOOMY FACE, KID?
SMILE!
HE WAS A FAMOUS MASTER SWORDSMAN NAMED ANDREAS WEBBER.
THUD
Gah ha!
OUT OF BREATH ALREADY?
AT THIS RATE, YOU'LL DIE HERE BEFORE YOU CAN DIE IN BATTLE.

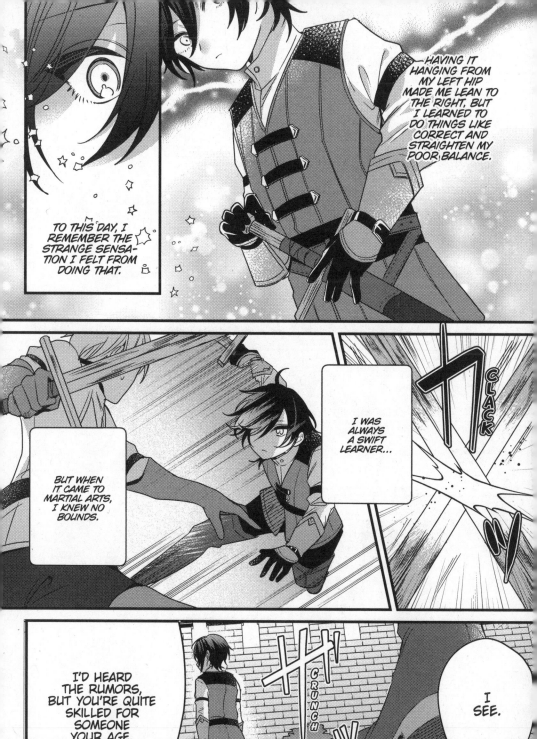

—HAVING IT HANGING FROM MY LEFT HIP MADE ME LEAN TO THE RIGHT, BUT I LEARNED TO DO THINGS LIKE CORRECT AND STRAIGHTEN MY POOR BALANCE.

TO THIS DAY, I REMEMBER THE STRANGE SENSATION I FELT FROM DOING THAT.

BUT WHEN IT CAME TO MARTIAL ARTS, I KNEW NO BOUNDS.

I WAS ALWAYS A SWIFT LEARNER...

CLACK

I'D HEARD THE RUMORS, BUT YOU'RE QUITE SKILLED FOR SOMEONE YOUR AGE.

CRUNCH

I SEE.

I HAD THE FULL SPECTRUM OF HUMAN EMOTIONS, BUT NOTHING STIRRED THEM FOR ME.
DO YOU LIKE THAT BOOK?
I WAS FULLY CAPABLE OF PHYSICALLY LAUGHING AND CRYING, BUT I COULD NEVER MANAGE THE EMOTIONAL SIDE.
COOL. LEND IT TO ME NEXT.
YES.
STILL, MY FAMILY AND SERVANTS SHOWERED ME WITH AFFECTION.
IN A WAY, IT FELT LIKE A WASTE.
AS THE SON OF A DUKE, I LEARNED AS MANY HELPFUL SKILLS AS POSSIBLE.
YOU HAVE SWORD FIGHTING PRACTICE THIS AFTERNOON.
SWORD...
I WAS FIVE WHEN I FIRST HELD A PRACTICE SWORD.

SHE WAS THE PINNACLE OF BEAUTY, DRAWING THE EYES OF EVERYONE AROUND HER.

HER SMILE WAS GENTLE AND BRIGHT.

THE SECOND PRINCE HAD HER ATTENTION.

HE COULD STAND BESIDE HER WITHOUT HESITATION.

I WANTED TO SCREAM THAT SHE WAS MINE SO BADLY, BUT I ENDURED.

I'VE KNOWN SOMETHING WAS WRONG WITH ME FOR AS A LONG AS I COULD REMEMBER.

I WAS SO DESPERATE TO HAVE HER, I COULD'VE KILLED THE MAN I WAS SUPPOSED TO PROTECT.

すーZZZ
すーZZZ…
I FINALLY HAVE YOU.
MY BELOVED.
Chapter 2
THIS HAS BEEN A LONG ROAD.
I'VE ENDURED FOR SO LONG.

THE VILLAINESS AND THE DEMON KNIGHT

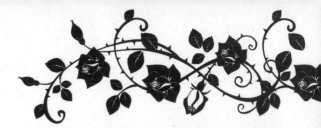

THE VILLAINESS AND THE DEMON KNIGHT

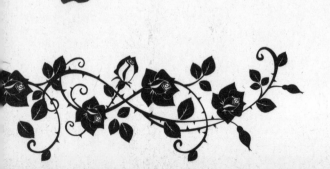

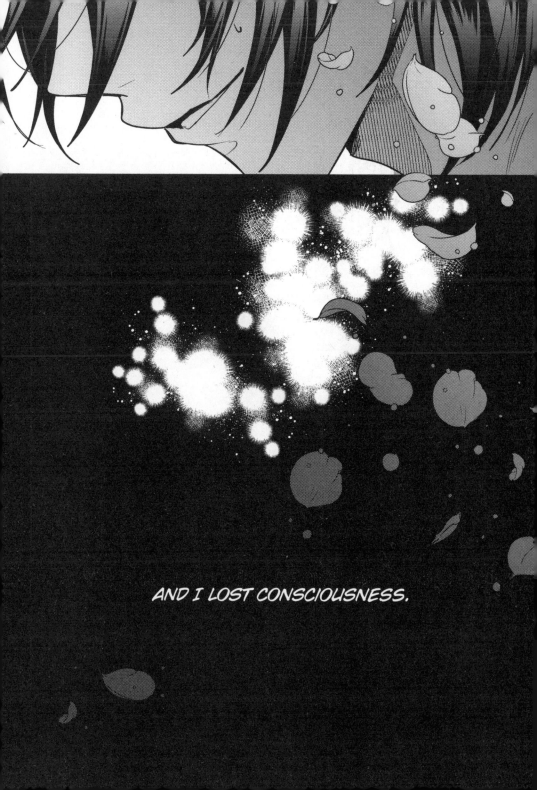

AND I LOST CONSCIOUSNESS.

SMACK
LORD LUKIE!
SMACK
SHLUP
PANT!
I CAN'T TAKE IT ANYMORE...
SHLUP
PANT!
SHLUP
IF YOU WANT TO STOP, THEN SWEAR...
THAT YOU ARE MINE.
IF YOU DO, I'LL FINISH.
I- I SWEAR IT! I'M YOURS!
I SWEAR THAT I'M YOURS AND YOURS ALONE, LORD LUKIE!
RIGHT AFTER I AN- SWERED, SOME- THING FLASHED...
FLASH

SMACK
Ah! Ah!
No!
SMACK
SHLAP
Ah!
SHLAP
Ah! Ah!
SHLAP
SMACK
Ah! Ah!
HE KEEPS CRAVING ME...
Ahn! I'm cumming again!
SMACK

IT'S UNBELIEV-ABLE THAT IT'D FEEL SO GOOD THAT HE COULDN'T HOLD BACK!
AND NOW HE'S SULKING AND HIDING HIS RED FACE!
HUG
I-I'M NOT SUPPOSED TO FEEL HAPPY OVER THIS!
THROB
...!
JUST NOW...
YOU GOT TIGHTER...
WH-WHAT IS IT, LORD LUKIE?
だら
SWEAT
だら
SWEAT
HEH HEH.
SMILE

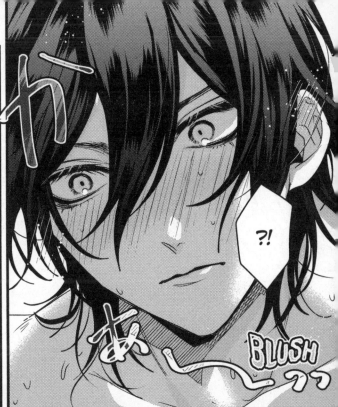

WHAT?

?!

YOU'RE
BLUSHING.

BLUSH

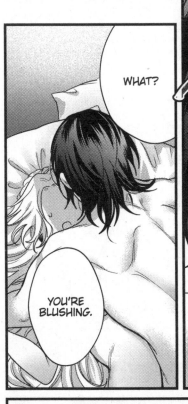

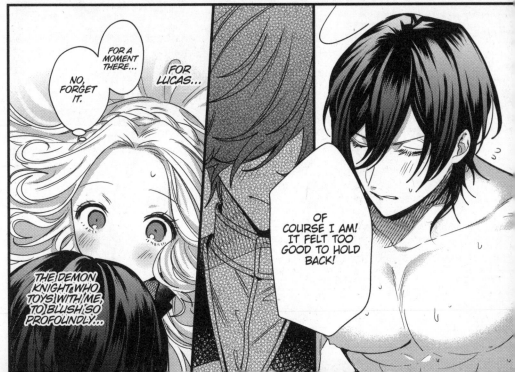

FOR A
MOMENT
THERE...

NO,
FORGET
IT.

FOR
LUCAS...

THE DEMON
KNIGHT WHO
TOYS WITH ME,
TO BLUSH SO
PROFOUNDLY...

OF
COURSE I AM!
IT FELT TOO
GOOD TO HOLD
BACK!

Mm.
Mm.
Mmmm-mm...
SPUURT
Tremble
TWITCH
QUIVER
QUIVER
TWITCH
Huff!
PANT...
PANT...
SLIDE
DRIP
TWITCH
TWITCH
PANT...
LORD... LUKIE...
W-WAS THAT AN... ORGASM?
PANT...

Ah!
Huff!
JIGGLE たぷっ
Ah!
はっ PANT...
ぱん SMACK
はっ PANT!
JIGGLE たぷっ
PRESS
You can't...
Ah!
ぱん SMACK
ずぷっ THRUST
ずぷっ THRUST
Ah!
Ah!
ぱん SMACK
ズヌッ THRUST
じゅぽっ SHLIP
Not there!
Ah! Ah!
じゅぽっ SHLIP
SHLUP
NGH...
Ah!
SHLUP
Ah.
SHLUP
Mm...
KISS ちゅ
ちゅ... KISS
SOME-THING'S...
COMING...

HERE! CAN YOU TELL HOW DEEP I AM?
ROCK
CLENCH
CLENCH
SHLUP
Mm...
Eep...
SHIVER
SHIVER
I CAN'T...
PANT...
TAKE IT.
PANT...
IT'S TOO BIG...
THIS IS SUCH A LOVELY VIEW, CECE.
MAY I BE ROUGHER?

MM. DON'T... MOVE...
OH YEAH, I'VE HEARD THAT TAKING SOMEONE'S VIRGINITY IS DIFFICULT FOR THE MAN, TOO.
?!
A-ARE YOU ALL RIGHT, LORD LUKIE?!
WHAT SHOULD I DO?
GOD DAMMIT!
SHOVE
KYAA!

I'M SUFFERING INSIDE. I NEED MORE PAIN.
PLEASE, LORD LUKIE. MORE.
GIVE ME...
......
HUH? LORD LUKIE?
SILENCE
し——ん...

!
TUG
CECE...
CECILIA...
MM. LORD LUKIE. LORD LUKIE...
HE'S TERRIBLE...
AND IT HURTS...
BUT I WANT MORE.
I WANT HIM TO FILL ME.
LORD LUKIE...

MY...
YOU ARE TRULY ADORABLE, CECE...
WHY?
WHEN HE SAYS MY NAME SO SWEETLY, IT'S ALMOST AS IF HIS GOLDEN EYES ARE SWIMMING WITH HAPPY TEARS.
HIS HANDS GRIP ME WITH THE STRENGTH OF SOMEONE WHO LOATHES ME, BUT HE'S GENTLE WHEN HE CARESSES MY CHEEK.
STILL. I'M A PROSTITUTE NOW, AND HE'S MY CUSTOMER.
HE DIDN'T COME HERE TO SLEEP WITH ME BECAUSE HE LOVES ME.
HE WANTS TO RUIN ME AND SAVE THE HEROINE.
STAB...

ぬるっ
SLIP
ぎち…
Squilch
MMMM.
WHAT IS THIS?!
IT'S HOT.
I CAN'T BREATHE!
TREMBLE
NGH. CECE... DON'T CLENCH AROUND ME SO HARD. IT FEELS TOO GOOD...
I WANT TO SAVOR YOU MORE...
SHIVER
HA HA...
Ah...
THRUST
Huff...
THRUST
THAT'S RIGHT. I'M THE ONLY ONE WHO CAN SATISFY YOU AND FILL YOUR WOMB.
I WILL STEAL YOUR VIRGINITY!
TO THINK MY SEED WILL FILL YOUR WOMB... THAT'S JUST...
Huff...
Ahhhh!
RAM
AH, THERE IS NO GREATER GIFT.

Huff...
Huff...
I'D BEEN DEBATING WHETHER TO BE GENTLE OR ROUGH RIGHT AWAY...
BUT I'D LIKE TO SAVOR YOUR FIRST TIME.
Huff...
PUSH
JOLT
TWITCH
TWITCH
EEP! NO!
I'LL BE GENTLE.
SLURCH
PANT...
IT HURTS, IT HURTS IT HURTS!
PANT...
PANT...
PANT...
PANT...
I IMAGINE IT IS QUITE PAINFUL...
BUT ONLY THIS ONE TIME.
ENDURE IT.

PUSH INSIDE YOU.
THRUST
WHAT? AH...
AHHH!
PANT...
HA HA! YOU'RE SO DAMN TIGHT... ARE YOU TRYING TO PUSH ME OUT? I CAN'T GET ENOUGH.
PANT...
TWITCH
I CAN'T WAIT TO HEAR YOU MOAN ONCE I START THRUSTING.
I'VE BEEN HOLDING BACK AND WAITING FOR YOU TO WAKE.
TWITCH

OH CECE, HURRY.
OPEN YOUR EYES...
ぱ
BLINK
OH! DID I?
ARE YOU AWAKE?
DID I LOSE CONSCIOUS-NESS?
LORD LUKIE?
DON'T GET UP.
I'M ABOUT TO...

TWITCH
Mm...
KISS
KISS
KISS
?!
CHOMP
NIBBLE
TWITCH
NIBBLE
OUCH! TH-THAT HURTS!
SLICH
N-NOOO!
Ah!
Ah!
SLICH
NIP
NIP
SLICH
SLICH
AHH!
SQUICH

U-UM... L-LORD LUKIE?
???
WAS I THAT MEAN TO THE HEROINE?
I'M TOO SCARED TO ASK...
SHOULD I BE SORRY FOR MAKING YOU ANXIOUS?
YOU'RE VERY KIND.
I SHALL INDULGE YOUR KINDNESS...
NOW, HOW SHOULD I LEAVE MY MARK TO PROVE YOU'RE MINE?
I FEEL LIKE HIS IDEA OF A "MARK" IS VERY DIFFERENT FROM MINE.
UM, WHAT WOULD YOU LIKE ME TO DO?
I'M TOO SCARED TO ASK HIM TO ELABORATE ON THAT!
JUST KEEP DOING WHAT YOU'RE DOING.

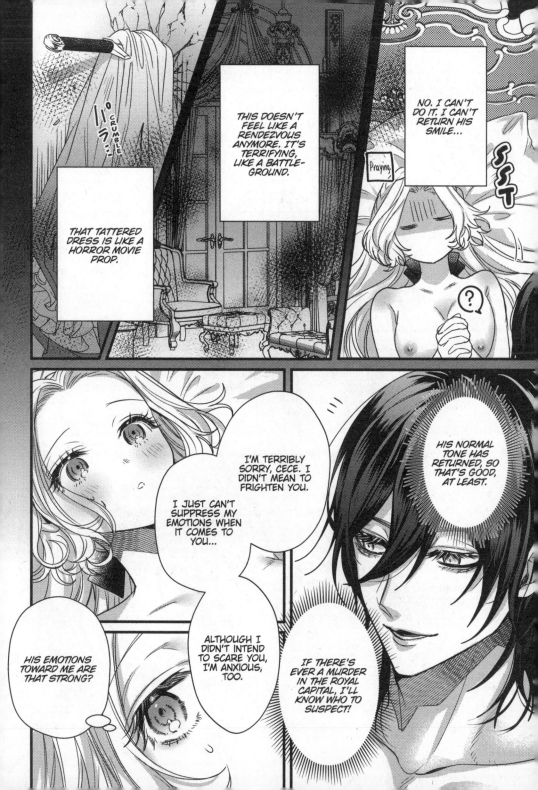

THAT TATTERED DRESS IS LIKE A HORROR MOVIE PROP.

THIS DOESN'T FEEL LIKE A RENDEZVOUS ANYMORE. IT'S TERRIFYING, LIKE A BATTLE-GROUND.

NO. I CAN'T DO IT. I CAN'T RETURN HIS SMILE...

Praying.

CRUMBLE

SST

?

I'M TERRIBLY SORRY, CECE. I DIDN'T MEAN TO FRIGHTEN YOU.

I JUST CAN'T SUPPRESS MY EMOTIONS WHEN IT COMES TO YOU...

HIS NORMAL TONE HAS RETURNED, SO THAT'S GOOD, AT LEAST.

HIS EMOTIONS TOWARD ME ARE THAT STRONG?

ALTHOUGH I DIDN'T INTEND TO SCARE YOU, I'M ANXIOUS, TOO.

IF THERE'S EVER A MURDER IN THE ROYAL CAPITAL, I'LL KNOW WHO TO SUSPECT!

H-HIS TONE CHANGED.
IT WASN'T DIRECTED TOWARD ANYONE SPECIFIC.
U-U-U-U-UM, YOU, L-LORD LUKIE...
HEH.
HA HA HA!
YES, OF COURSE. NATURALLY YOU WOULD ASK ME FOR HELP.
はぁ…
SIGH...
I THOUGHT YOU WERE THINKING OF SOMEONE ELSE WHILE I WAS INSIDE YOU...
SNEER
I WAS THINKING I'D HAVE TO ELIMINATE WHOEVER YOU WERE THINKING ABOUT.

RUMBLE
RUMBLE
CECE, WHAT DID YOU JUST SAY?
RUMBLE
RUMBLE
DID I MISHEAR? YOU SAID *HELP ME.*
UH! I DIDN'T ...
EEEK!
HELP YOU?
WHO WERE YOU TALKING TO?
WELL?

STAB
?!
SHLUCK
TH-THAT HURTS...
HEH HEH. I GOT TWO FINGERS INSIDE.
SO THIS IS WHAT YOUR PUSSY FEELS LIKE...
IT FELT SO GOOD BEFORE THIS.
BUT NOW, IT HURTS...
HE REALLY IS A DEMON!
NO...
HELP ME...

もにゅっ FONDLE
むにゅっ FONDLE
S-SEE WHAT?
へっ SLURP
HYA!
ふっ
れろ~っ LICK
Ah...
Ah.
Mm...
Ah.
ちぃ SUCK
Ah.
ゆっ
PANT... はーっ
B-BREASTS CAN GO THAT FAR INSIDE A MOUTH?
HOW CAN LUMPS OF FLESH BE SO SENSITIVE?!
はーっ PANT...
トロ～ MELT
Ahn!
Ah!
YOU'RE HARD LIKE A LITTLE BEAN DOWN HERE... ARE YOU FEELING IT?
STOP EXPLAINING EVERYTHING!
ぐちゅっ SQUICH
IF I TEASE YOU WITH MY THUMB, YOUR HONEY OVERFLOWS... I CAN'T GET ENOUGH...
ぐちゅっ SQUICH
NO, NO! YOU CAN'T! DON'T TEASE ME--
くちゅっ SQUICH
Mm!
ぐちゅっ SQUICH
クチュ SQUICH
AHH! DON'T!

DOES BEING WATCHED TURN YOU ON, CECE?
N-NO!
HYAAN!
Twitch Twitch
OH?
SQUICH
YOU'VE GOTTEN WETTER, CECE.
YOUR CUTE LOWER LIPS ARE DROOLING WITH HAPPINESS OVER THE FACT THAT I'M WATCHING...
SQUICH
shiver
SQUICH
SEE? THEY'RE MAKING LEWD NOISES.
shiver
SQUICH
NO...
SQUICH
OH, I SEE.

F
KYAA!
WUD
TUG
FLAP
HUH?
L-LORD LUKIE?!
CLINK
HE TORE HIS BELT TOO?!
CECE...
SPREAD YOUR LEGS.

YOU'RE DRIPPING WITH HONEY.
DRIP
YOU GET WET EASILY, CECE.
...!
Blush
NO MORE...
PLIP
LORD LUKIE...
PLIP
DON'T SAY THOSE THINGS...
...!
CECILIA!

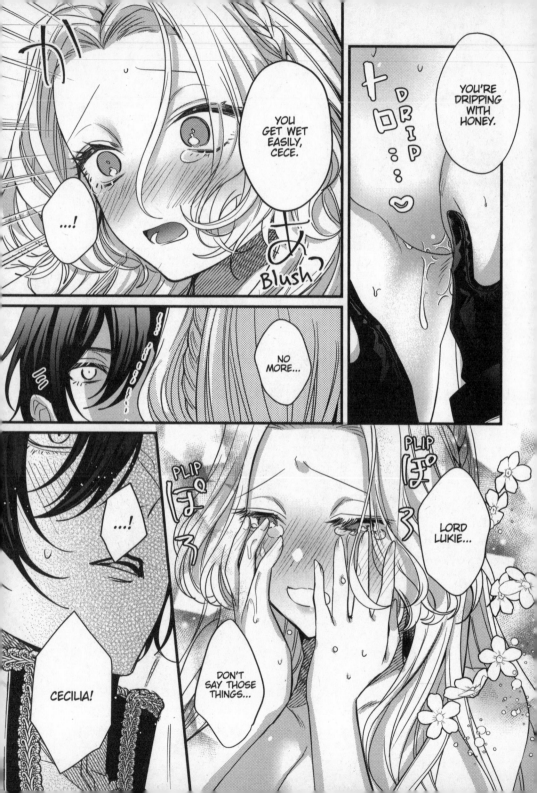

SUCK
LORD...
LUKIE!
TREMBLE
TREMBLE
I CAN'T DO THIS!
LORD LUKIE!
PUSH
SUCK
SUCK
BLEH
TWITCH
EEP! I'M GOING TO--
AH!
TWITCH
TWITCH
SLURP
LICK
LICK

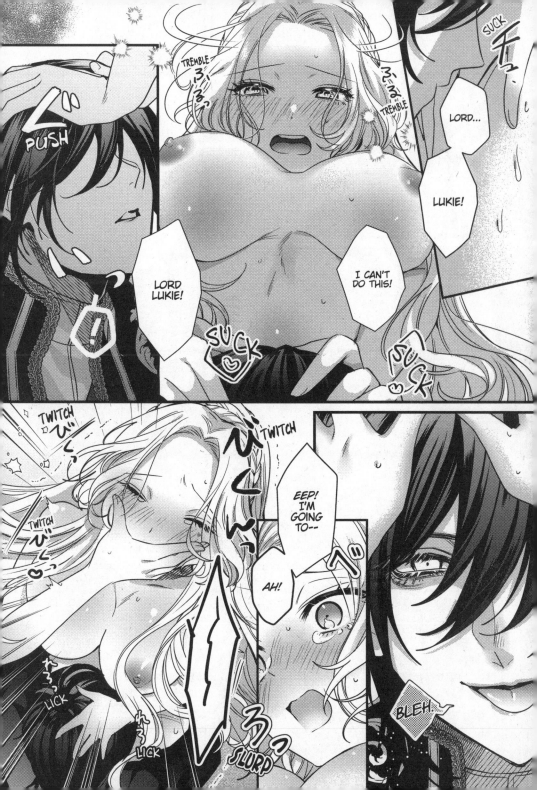

WHAT AM I DOING, BOLDLY JUSTIFYING MY REASON FOR BEING NUDE WHILE COMPLETELY NAKED?!
FAIR...
SOFT...
WHISPER
THIN...
EEP!
THE SAME COLOR AS YOUR HAIR...
PANT
D-DON'T SAY--
EEEEK!
SUCK

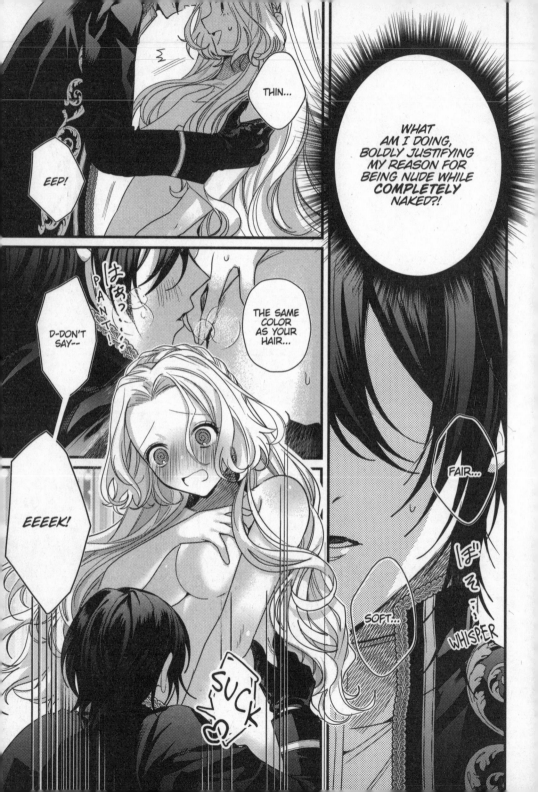

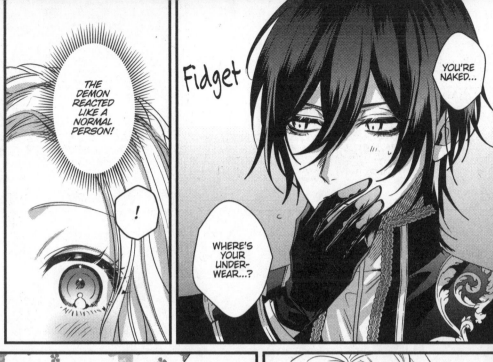

THE DEMON REACTED LIKE A NORMAL PERSON!

Fidget

YOU'RE NAKED...

WHERE'S YOUR UNDER-WEAR...?

!

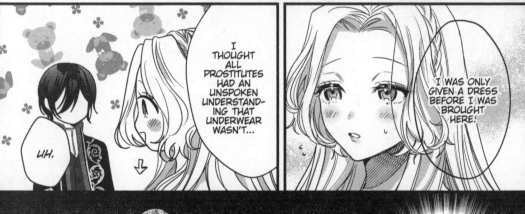

UH.

I THOUGHT ALL PROSTITUTES HAD AN UNSPOKEN UNDERSTAND-ING THAT UNDERWEAR WASN'T...

I WAS ONLY GIVEN A DRESS BEFORE I WAS BROUGHT HERE!

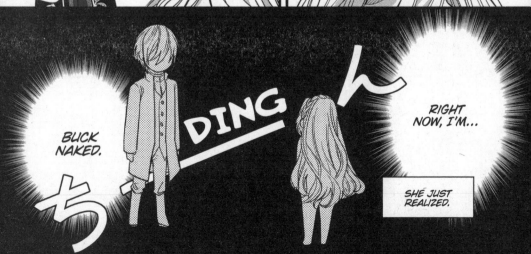

BUCK NAKED.

DING

RIGHT NOW, I'M...

SHE JUST REALIZED.

ALL RIGHT, CECE.
I'M GOING TO MAKE LOVE TO YOU NOW.
......
UM...

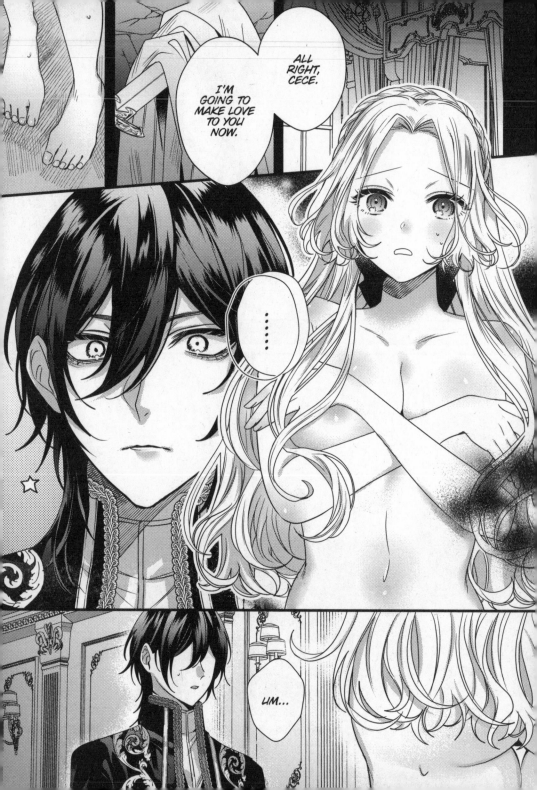

ALL RIGHT, CECE.
I'M GOING TO MAKE LOVE TO YOU NOW.

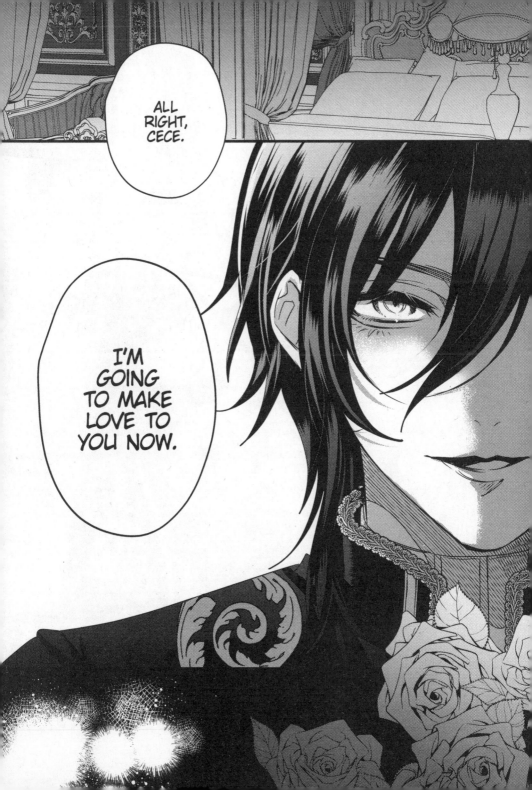

GODDESS, BUDDHA, MOTHER, FATHER, I'M SO SORRY.
PLEASE FORGIVE MY EARLY DEATH...
......
WHAM
ばっ
FLUTTER
?!
DID... DID HE JUST...
STAB THE WALL?!
SWISH

TAKE IT OFF IMMEDIATELY.
HE REALLY WILL...
OH.
OKAY.
KILL ME THIS TIME!!
ガク SHAKE
ガク SHAKE

SST
TAKE IT OFF.
DON'T WORRY. I WILL BUY YOU A NEW DRESS.
I CAN'T JUST--
TAP
SLASH
!!!
WHAT...
JUST HAPPENED?

HUH?
CLANG

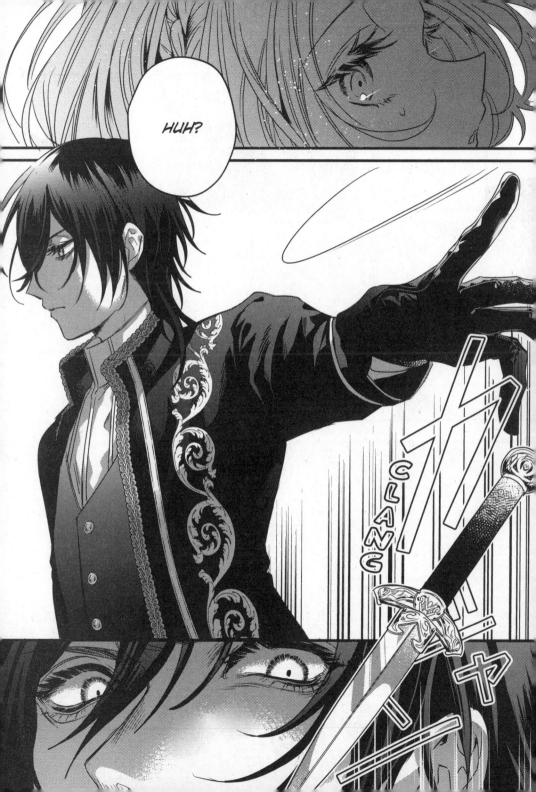

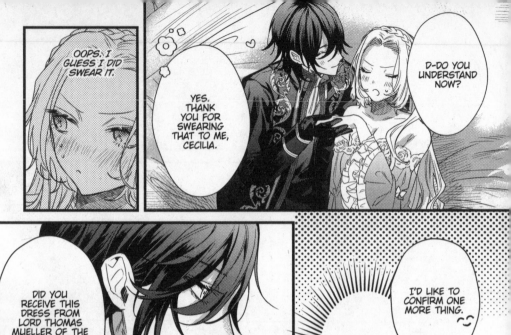

OOPS. I GUESS I DID SWEAR IT.

YES. THANK YOU FOR SWEARING THAT TO ME, CECILIA.

D-DO YOU UNDERSTAND NOW?

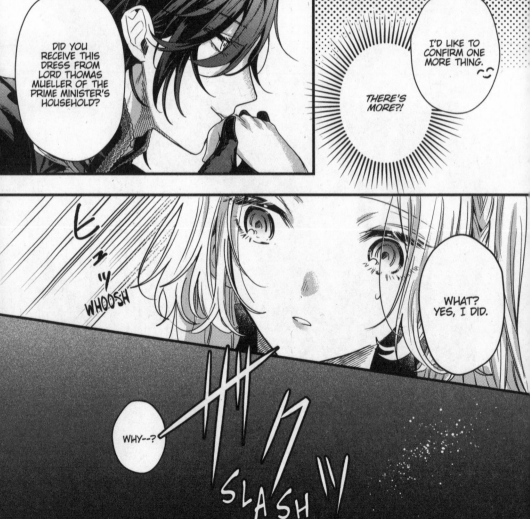

DID YOU RECEIVE THIS DRESS FROM LORD THOMAS MUELLER OF THE PRIME MINISTER'S HOUSEHOLD?

THERE'S MORE?!

I'D LIKE TO CONFIRM ONE MORE THING.

WHAT? YES, I DID.

WHY--?

WHOOSH

SLASH

TREMBLE
ふる

TREMBLE
ふる

DON'T BE ANGRY, CECE.

I'M NOT SWEARING ANYTHING TO YOU!

I MERELY WISH TO CONFIRM...

B-BUT THESE THINGS... K-KISSING AND TOUCHING OR ANYTHING MORE...

WHETHER ANYONE HAS TOUCHED YOU.

カ
BLUSH

ああ

I'VE ONLY EVER DONE THEM JUST NOW WITH YOU...

ぱ

WHY IS HE SMILING SO BRIGHTLY?

OH CECE...

ああ

BEAM

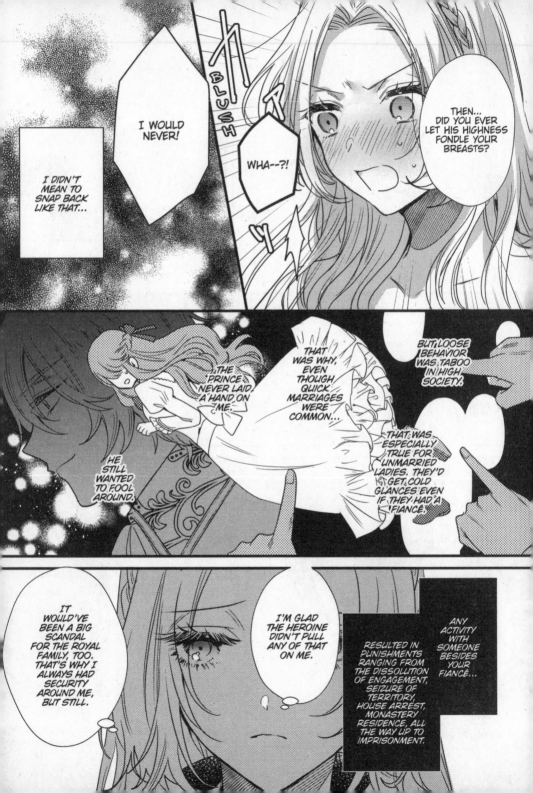

THEN... DID YOU EVER LET HIS HIGHNESS FONDLE YOUR BREASTS?

WHA--?!

I WOULD NEVER!

I DIDN'T MEAN TO SNAP BACK LIKE THAT...

BLUSH

THE PRINCE NEVER LAID A HAND ON ME.

HE STILL WANTED TO FOOL AROUND.

THAT WAS WHY, EVEN THOUGH QUICK MARRIAGES WERE COMMON...

BUT, LOOSE BEHAVIOR WAS TABOO IN HIGH SOCIETY.

THAT WAS ESPECIALLY TRUE FOR UNMARRIED LADIES. THEY'D GET COLD GLANCES EVEN IF THEY HAD A FIANCÉ.

IT WOULD'VE BEEN A BIG SCANDAL FOR THE ROYAL FAMILY, TOO. THAT'S WHY I ALWAYS HAD SECURITY AROUND ME, BUT STILL.

I'M GLAD THE HEROINE DIDN'T PULL ANY OF THAT ON ME.

ANY ACTIVITY WITH SOMEONE BESIDES YOUR FIANCÉ...

RESULTED IN PUNISHMENTS RANGING FROM THE DISSOLUTION OF ENGAGEMENT, SEIZURE OF TERRITORY, HOUSE ARREST, MONASTERY RESIDENCE, ALL THE WAY UP TO IMPRISONMENT.

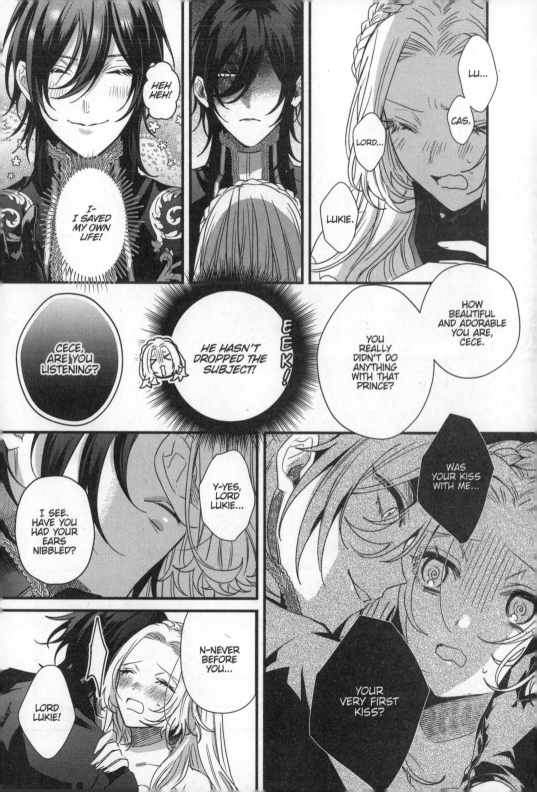

HEH HEH!

LU...

CAS.

LORD...

LUKIE.

I— I SAVED MY OWN LIFE!

CECE, ARE YOU LISTENING?

HE HASN'T DROPPED THE SUBJECT!

EEK!

YOU REALLY DIDN'T DO ANYTHING WITH THAT PRINCE?

HOW BEAUTIFUL AND ADORABLE YOU ARE, CECE.

Y-YES, LORD LUKIE...

I SEE. HAVE YOU HAD YOUR EARS NIBBLED?

WAS YOUR KISS WITH ME...

N-NEVER BEFORE YOU...

LORD LUKIE!

YOUR VERY FIRST KISS?

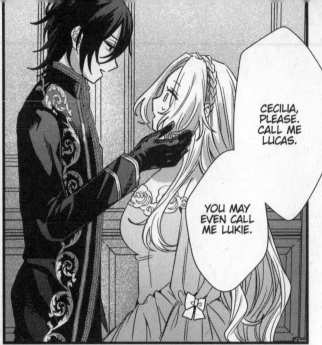

CECILIA, PLEASE. CALL ME LUCAS.

YOU MAY EVEN CALL ME LUKIE.

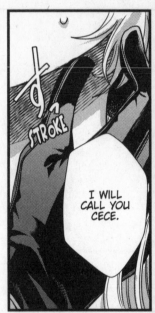

♪ STROKE

I WILL CALL YOU CECE.

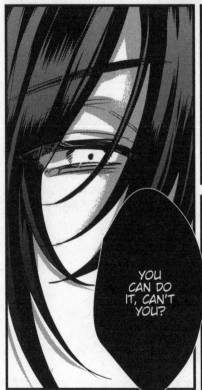

YOU CAN DO IT, CAN'T YOU?

GO ON, CECE. SAY MY NAME.

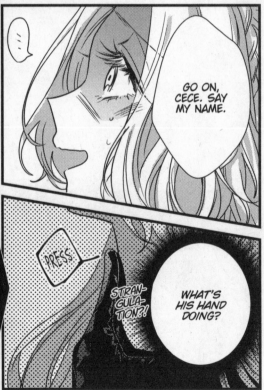

PRESS!

STRAN-GULA-TION?!

WHAT'S HIS HAND DOING?

CAN YOU SWEAR ON YOUR HOUSEHOLD?
MY HOUSEHOLD?
IS HE TALKING ABOUT AN OATH AMONG NOBLES?
AN OATH WHERE IF I LIE, EVEN MY FAMILY'S VASSALS WILL BE EXECUTED AND I CAN'T COMPLAIN?
B-DMP
B-DMP
WHY MUST I SWEAR THAT THIS IS MY FIRST KISS IN THE FIRST PLACE?
I'M NOT EVEN A MEMBER OF THE CLINE FAMILY ANYMORE.
I DON'T HAVE THE INFLUENCE TO MAKE A NOBLE OATH.
B-DMP
CLAP
U-UM...
BUT I CAN'T TELL HIM THAT!!
OH, I KNOW!
HUH?

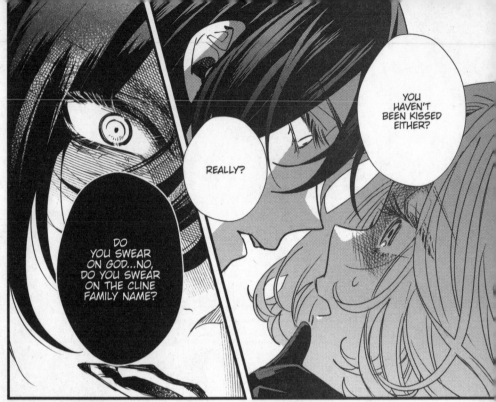

YOU HAVEN'T BEEN KISSED EITHER?

REALLY?

DO YOU SWEAR ON GOD...NO, DO YOU SWEAR ON THE CLINE FAMILY NAME?

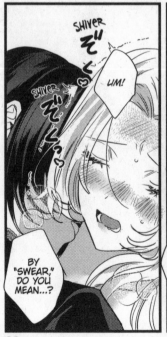

SHIVER

SHIVER

UM!

BY "SWEAR," DO YOU MEAN...?

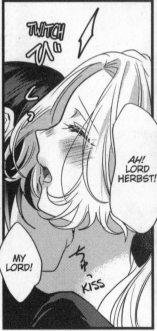

TWITCH

AH! LORD HERBST!

MY LORD!

KISS

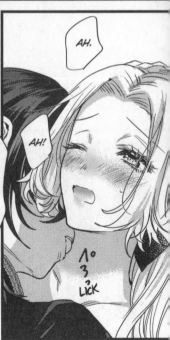

AH.

AH!

LICK

21

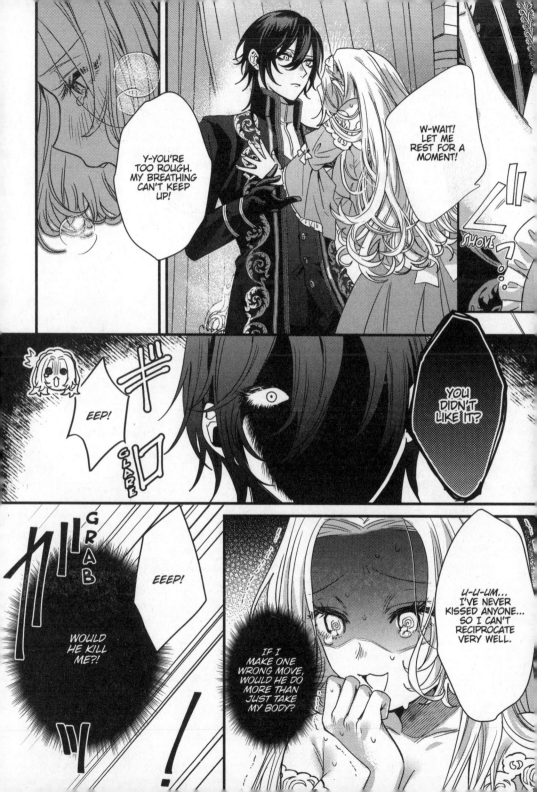

Y-YOU'RE TOO ROUGH. MY BREATHING CAN'T KEEP UP!

W-WAIT! LET ME REST FOR A MOMENT!

SHOVE

EEP!

GLARE

YOU DIDN'T LIKE IT?

GRAB

EEEP!

WOULD HE KILL ME?!

IF I MAKE ONE WRONG MOVE, WOULD HE DO MORE THAN JUST TAKE MY BODY?

U-U-UM... I'VE NEVER KISSED ANYONE... SO I CAN'T RECIPROCATE VERY WELL.

SIGH...
AT LONG LAST!
U...
UM...
MM?!
WHAT'S GOING ON?!
PULL
MM...
NH...
MMM.
HAA!

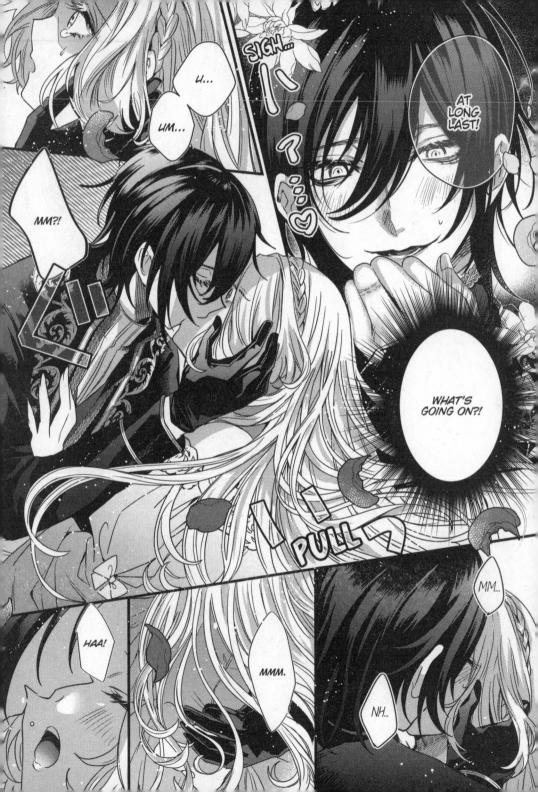

CHOMP
AND MAKE IT HURT ON PURPOSE.
OUCH!
SHUDDER
THAT HURTS, MY LORD...
FINALLY...
I FINALLY HAVE YOU, CECILIA.
AHH!
NIBBLE
NIBBLE
WHA...?

DON'T YOU WORRY. JUST RELAX, CECILIA.
I'LL BE GENTLE.
I WON'T HURT YOU... *BEYOND THE FIRST TIME.*
SMILE
I CAN'T RELAX AT ALL.
ISN'T HE SUPPOSED TO SAY HE'LL MAKE SURE IT DOESN'T HURT THE FIRST TIME??
SO, MY FIRST TIME *WILL* HURT...
HMM.
THAT DOES SEEM TO BE THE GENERAL CONSEN-SUS.
I COULD GIVE YOU SOME MEDICINE TO MAKE SURE IT DOESN'T, THOUGH.
MEDICINE?
AN APHRODISIAC?
BUT IF IT EASES THE ,PAIN, I SUPPOSE I SHOULD USE IT.
BUT...
AS THE MAN WHO TAKES YOUR VIRGINITY, I WANT TO LEAVE MY MARK...

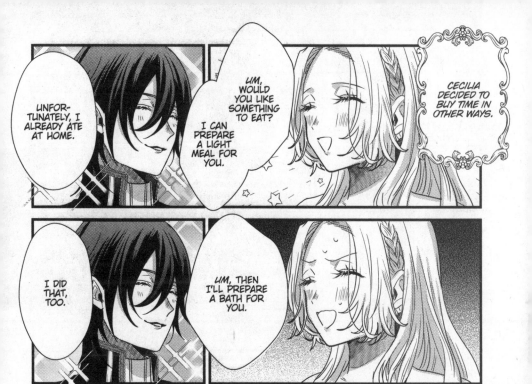

UNFORTUNATELY, I ALREADY ATE AT HOME.

UM, WOULD YOU LIKE SOMETHING TO EAT? I CAN PREPARE A LIGHT MEAL FOR YOU.

CECILIA DECIDED TO BUY TIME IN OTHER WAYS.

I DID THAT, TOO.

UM, THEN I'LL PREPARE A BATH FOR YOU.

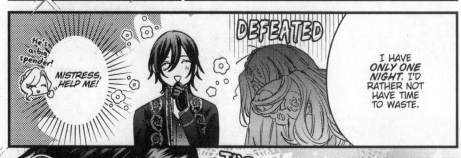

DEFEATED

He's a big spender!

MISTRESS, HELP ME!

I HAVE ONLY ONE NIGHT. I'D RATHER NOT HAVE TIME TO WASTE.

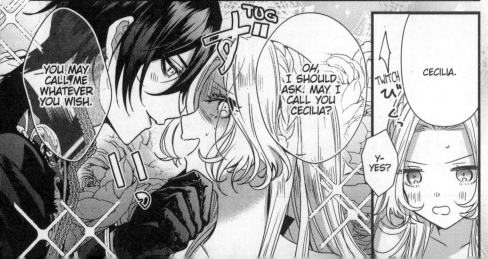

TUG

YOU MAY CALL ME WHATEVER YOU WISH.

OH, I SHOULD ASK. MAY I CALL YOU CECILIA?

CECILIA.

TWITCH

Y-YES?

BUT ALAS, THERE WAS NO WAY AROUND IT THIS TIME.
I USED THE FULL EXTENT OF MY NAME AND MY FAMILY'S POWER TO BEND THE RULES.
Repulsed.
AT A BROTHEL?!
I DON'T KNOW WHAT HE'S PLOTTING...
I...I UNDER-STAND THE SITUATION...
AND I DON'T WANT TO GIVE HIM A WHOLE NIGHT. BUT HE HAS ME FOR WHATEVER HE WANTS TONIGHT.
THINK ABOUT IT, THOUGH.
A DELICATE MARQUISE AND A BURLY KNIGHT? TOGETHER FOR THE WHOLE NIGHT? WON'T I DIE?
IS HE GOING TO FUCK ME TO DEATH?!
THAT'S A SHAMEFUL WAY TO GO.
I REFUSE TO DIE DURING INTERCOURSE!

WAIT, WHAT WAS THAT? A FLASHBACK MONTAGE?
I NEVER EXPECTED THE KNIGHT OF THE BLUE ROSE TO FREQUENT THIS PLACE, TOO!
ANYWAY, THIS BROTHEL IS FAMOUS FOR CATERING TO NOBLES.
SECOND NAME: KNIGHT OF THE BLUE ROSE
HE SHOULDN'T NEED TO COME TO A BROTHEL, THOUGH. HE'S PLENTY POPULAR!
ALL THAT BEING SAID, I DON'T THINK I'VE DONE ANYTHING IN PARTICULAR FOR HIM TO SEEK REVENGE AGAINST ME.
I DIDN'T, DID I?!
I DON'T THINK I DID.
STILL, THOUGH!!
I'VE NEVER ABUSED MY TITLE BEFORE...

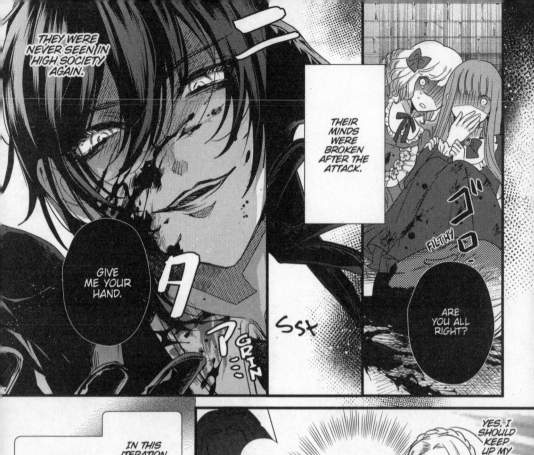

THEY WERE NEVER SEEN IN HIGH SOCIETY AGAIN.

THEIR MINDS WERE BROKEN AFTER THE ATTACK.

GIVE ME YOUR HAND.

FILTHY

Ssr

GRIN

ARE YOU ALL RIGHT?

BESIDES, I DETEST VULGARITY. AS A PRINCE'S CONSORT, THERE'S NO UPSIDE TO ME COMMITTING HIGH-SOCIETY TABOOS.

IN THIS ITERATION OF THE GAME, THOUGH, I DIDN'T ATTEND THAT EVENING'S PARTY DUE TO A COLD.

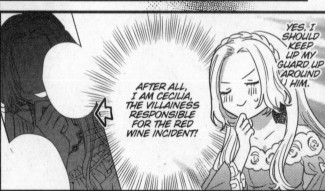

YES, I SHOULD KEEP UP MY GUARD UP AROUND HIM.

AFTER ALL, I AM CECILIA, THE VILLAINESS RESPONSIBLE FOR THE RED WINE INCIDENT!

THERE'S NO TIME FOR RELIEF WITH HIM HERE!

REMEMBER WHERE YOU ARE!

I'M SO GLAD THAT INCIDENT NEVER HAPPENED.

PHEW!

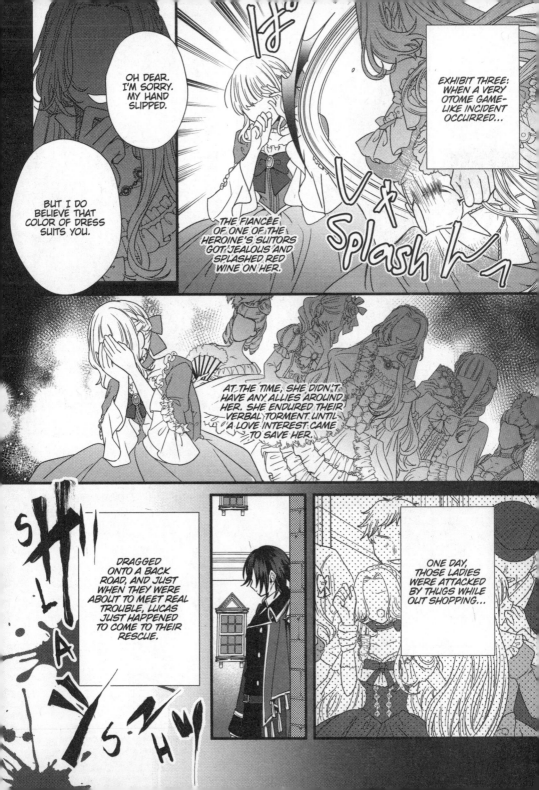

OH DEAR. I'M SORRY. MY HAND SLIPPED.

BUT I DO BELIEVE THAT COLOR OF DRESS SUITS YOU.

EXHIBIT THREE: WHEN A VERY OTOME GAME-LIKE INCIDENT OCCURRED...

THE FIANCÉE OF ONE OF THE HEROINE'S SUITORS GOT JEALOUS AND SPLASHED RED WINE ON HER.

AT THE TIME, SHE DIDN'T HAVE ANY ALLIES AROUND HER. SHE ENDURED THEIR VERBAL TORMENT UNTIL A LOVE INTEREST CAME TO SAVE HER.

DRAGGED ONTO A BACK ROAD, AND JUST WHEN THEY WERE ABOUT TO MEET REAL TROUBLE, LUCAS JUST HAPPENED TO COME TO THEIR RESCUE.

ONE DAY, THOSE LADIES WERE ATTACKED BY THUGS WHILE OUT SHOPPING...

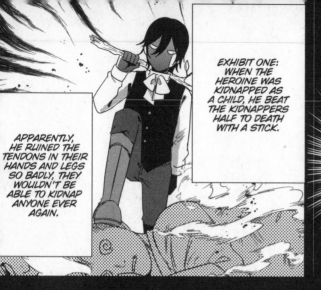

APPARENTLY, HE RUINED THE TENDONS IN THEIR HANDS AND LEGS SO BADLY, THEY WOULDN'T BE ABLE TO KIDNAP ANYONE EVER AGAIN.

EXHIBIT ONE: WHEN THE HEROINE WAS KIDNAPPED AS A CHILD, HE BEAT THE KIDNAPPERS HALF TO DEATH WITH A STICK.

HE'S THE PERFECT SUPERHUMAN. SO WHY DO I CALL HIM A DEMON?

WELL, BECAUSE HE'S ABNORMALLY RUTHLESS TOWARD THE HEROINE'S ENEMIES.

HE WAS FOUND IN A RESTROOM COMPLETELY NAKED AND BOUND WITH ROPE.

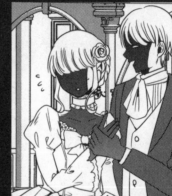

EXHIBIT TWO: WHEN A CERTAIN DUKE MADE PASSES AT HER AT AN EVENING PARTY...

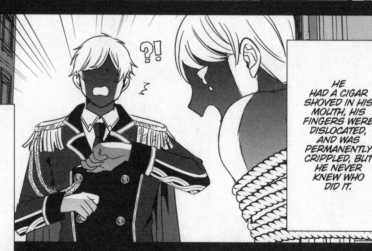

(HE DID HAVE A NEWFOUND FEAR OF THE IMPERIAL ORDER UNIFORM, HOWEVER.)

HE HAD A CIGAR SHOVED IN HIS MOUTH, HIS FINGERS WERE DISLOCATED, AND WAS PERMANENTLY CRIPPLED, BUT HE NEVER KNEW WHO DID IT.

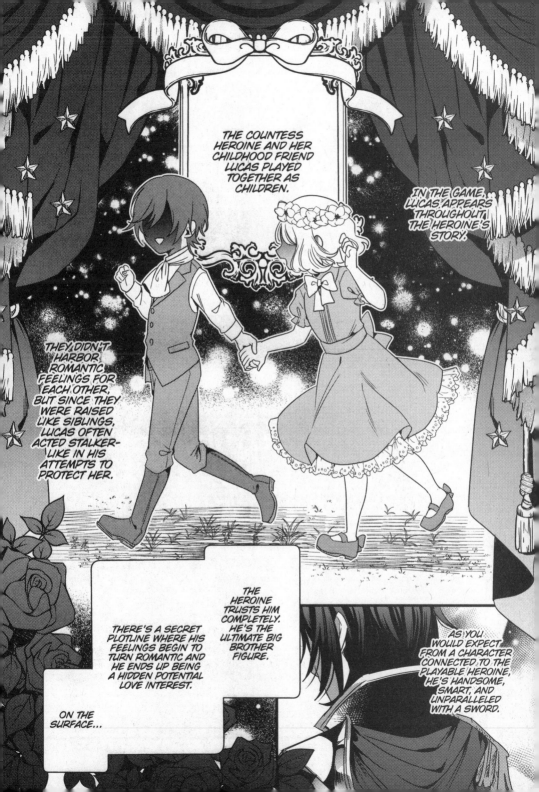

THE COUNTESS HEROINE AND HER CHILDHOOD FRIEND LUCAS PLAYED TOGETHER AS CHILDREN.

IN THE GAME, LUCAS APPEARS THROUGHOUT THE HEROINE'S STORY.

THEY DIDN'T HARBOR ROMANTIC FEELINGS FOR EACH OTHER, BUT SINCE THEY WERE RAISED LIKE SIBLINGS, LUCAS OFTEN ACTED STALKER-LIKE IN HIS ATTEMPTS TO PROTECT HER.

THE HEROINE TRUSTS HIM COMPLETELY. HE'S THE ULTIMATE BIG BROTHER FIGURE.

THERE'S A SECRET PLOTLINE WHERE HIS FEELINGS BEGIN TO TURN ROMANTIC AND HE ENDS UP BEING A HIDDEN POTENTIAL LOVE INTEREST.

AS YOU WOULD EXPECT FROM A CHARACTER CONNECTED TO THE PLAYABLE HEROINE, HE'S HANDSOME, SMART, AND UNPARALLELED WITH A SWORD.

ON THE SURFACE...

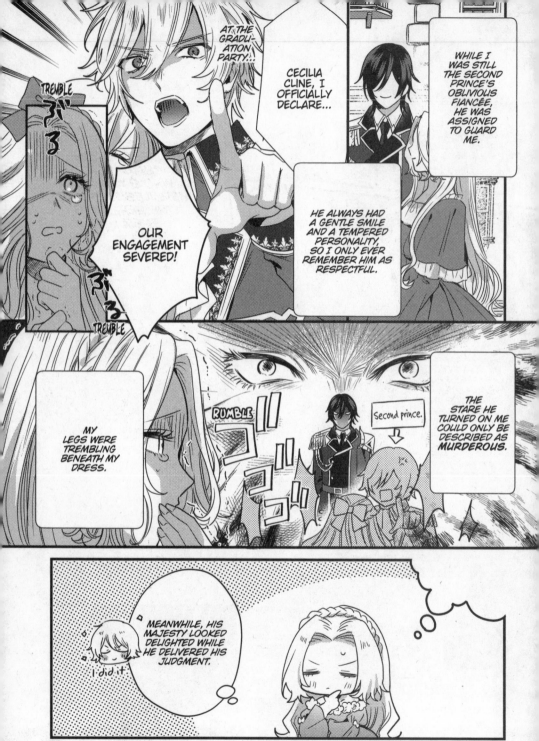

AT THE GRADUATION PARTY...

CECILIA CLINE, I OFFICIALLY DECLARE...

OUR ENGAGEMENT SEVERED!

TREMBLE

TREMBLE

WHILE I WAS STILL THE SECOND PRINCE'S OBLIVIOUS FIANCÉE, HE WAS ASSIGNED TO GUARD ME.

HE ALWAYS HAD A GENTLE SMILE AND A TEMPERED PERSONALITY, SO I ONLY EVER REMEMBER HIM AS RESPECTFUL.

MY LEGS WERE TREMBLING BENEATH MY DRESS.

RUMBLE

Second prince.

THE STARE HE TURNED ON ME COULD ONLY BE DESCRIBED AS MURDEROUS.

MEANWHILE, HIS MAJESTY LOOKED DELIGHTED WHILE HE DELIVERED HIS JUDGMENT.

I did it.

SECOND SON OF THE HERBST DUKEDOM AND VICE-CAPTAIN OF THE IMPERIAL ORDER, LUCAS HERBST.

Ho ho ho...

DUKE HERBST'S SON? THIS BROTHEL HAS TIME LIMITS. YOU CANNOT PAY BY THE NIGHT.

WHY IS MY FIRST CUSTOMER THE CLOSET DEMON CHARACTER WHO'S ALWAYS MERCILESS TOWARD THE HEROINE'S ENEMIES?!

YES, I'M AWARE.

I NEGO-TIATED AND PURCHASED A FULL NIGHT.

HIS MOTHER IS THE KING'S SISTER, WHICH MEANS HE'S PART OF THE LINE OF SUCCESSION. HOWEVER, AS THE SECOND SON, HE SET HIS SIGHTS ON KNIGHTHOOD WITH THE IMPERIAL ORDER AND ENTERED THE ACADEMY AT ONLY FIFTEEN.

SMILE

SMILE

AT EIGHTEEN, HE WAS BROUGHT INTO THE IMPERIAL ORDER AND TASKED WITH PROTECTING THE ROYAL FAMILY. ONE YEAR LATER, HIS GENIUS EARNED HIM THE ROLE OF VICE-CAPTAIN.

MAYBE THE HEROINE PICKED UP ON THE PRINCE'S DISTURBING THOUGHTS BECAUSE SHE SECRETLY INTERVENED BY CRYING TO THE PRIME MINISTER'S SON, WHO GOT ME SENT TO A BROTHEL.
I'LL INTRODUCE YOU TO A MUCH BETTER JOB THAN WHAT YOU'D FIND AT THE MONASTERY.
HMM.
A VIRGIN...
YOU MUST REALLY NEED THE MONEY.
WELL, THIS IS A HIGH-CLASS BROTHEL. I'D MORE THAN WELCOME AN EDUCATED GIRL.
THE MISTRESS LOOKED AT ME WITH PITY. THAT HURT.
WE HAVE MANY DIFFICULT CUSTOMERS. ARE YOU SURE ABOUT THIS?
AND THAT'S HOW I WENT FROM NUN TO HIGH-CLASS PROSTITUTE!
YES. I'M USED TO DIFFICULT PEOPLE.
Former consort of a prince
CECILIA, YOU HAVE YOUR FIRST JOB ALREADY.
WHAT?
BY "BLUE ROSE," DO YOU MEAN?!
THE KNIGHT OF THE BLUE ROSE REQUESTED YOU PERSONALLY. GOOD FOR YOU.
WHY...?

AS THE SECOND PRINCE'S FIANCÉE, I CREATED A CLIQUE AT SCHOOL AND ALIENATED THE HEROINE...

Heroine

AND NEVER INVITED HER TO TEA OR ANYTHING!

WHEN I DIDN'T HAVE MY MEMORIES, I DEFINITELY COMPLAINED A LOT AS CECILIA.

NOW THAT I THINK ABOUT IT, IT DOESN'T MAKE SENSE FOR A MAN WHO ISN'T MY FIANCÉ TO GET AWAY WITH PUTTING HIS HANDS ON ME, DOES IT?

WHICH ULTIMATELY LED TO ME GETTING SENT TO A MONASTERY.

THAT'S WHY THE FIRST PRINCE, WHO LOVED THE HEROINE, HATED ME SO MUCH...

SCREEECH!

WHAT A SCUM-BAG!

THAT DEADBEAT MUST'VE SEEN ME AS POTENTIAL DEAD WEIGHT AND WAS LOOKING FOR ANY EXCUSE TO GET RID OF ME.

Loves his side chicks.

ALL MY ACTUAL FIANCÉ COULD DO TO ME, A MARQUISE, WAS BREAK OFF THE ENGAGEMENT.

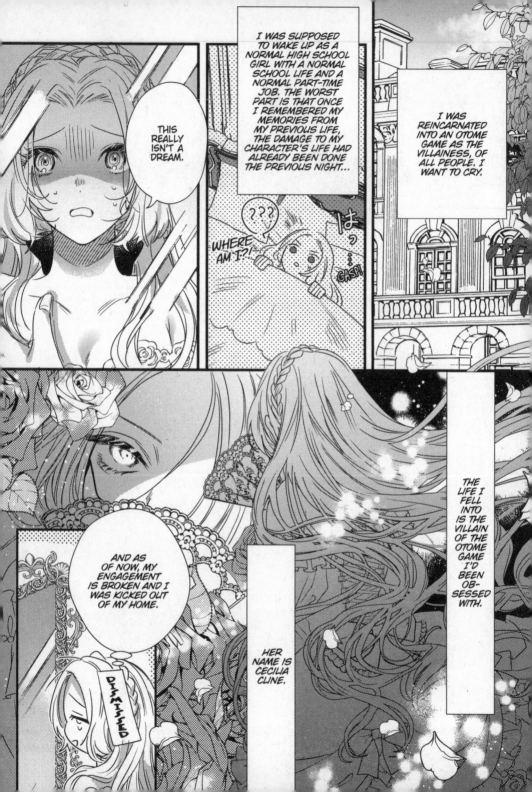

THIS REALLY ISN'T A DREAM.

I WAS SUPPOSED TO WAKE UP AS A NORMAL HIGH SCHOOL GIRL WITH A NORMAL SCHOOL LIFE AND A NORMAL PART-TIME JOB. THE WORST PART IS THAT ONCE I REMEMBERED MY MEMORIES FROM MY PREVIOUS LIFE, THE DAMAGE TO MY CHARACTER'S LIFE HAD ALREADY BEEN DONE THE PREVIOUS NIGHT...

???

WHERE AM I?!

GASP!

I WAS REINCARNATED INTO AN OTOME GAME AS THE VILLAINESS, OF ALL PEOPLE. I WANT TO CRY.

THE LIFE I FELL INTO IS THE VILLAIN OF THE OTOME GAME I'D BEEN OB-SESSED WITH.

AND AS OF NOW, MY ENGAGEMENT IS BROKEN AND I WAS KICKED OUT OF MY HOME.

HER NAME IS CECILIA CLINE.

DISMISSED

CECILIA...

I AM HERE...

YOU DIDN'T.

HEH.

TO PURCHASE A NIGHT WITH YOU.

DID I...

SMILE PROPERLY JUST NOW?

DEEP BLUE HAIR, THE COLOR OF A DUSK SKY.
EYES THE GOLDEN COLOR OF HONEY.
A CHARCOAL SUIT COMPLEMENTING HIS UNMATCHED BEAUTY...
GOOD DAY, LUCAS HERBST, SON OF THE DUKE.
I ASSUME YOU'VE COME ALL THIS WAY FOR AN IMPORTANT REASON.
WILL YOU REPEAT WHAT YOU SAID? I MIGHT'VE MISHEARD.
Chapter 1

CONTENTS

THE VILLAINESS AND THE DEMON KNIGHT
1

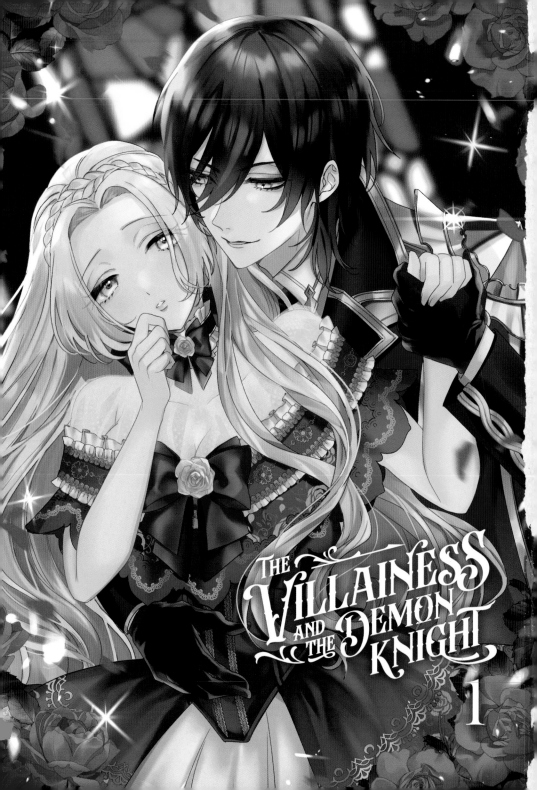